Monolingualism of the Other;
or,
The Prosthesis of Origin

Cultural Memory
in
the
Present

Mieke Bal and Hent de Vries, Editors

Monolingualism of the Other;
    or,
The Prosthesis of Origin

JACQUES DERRIDA

Translated by Patrick Mensah

Stanford University Press
Stanford, California

Assistance for the translation was provided
by the French Ministry of Culture

*Monolingualism of the Other; or, The Prosthesis
of Origin* was originally published in French
in 1996 under the title *Le monolinguisme de
l'autre: ou la prothèse d'origine.*
© 1996 by Editions Galilée

Stanford University Press, Stanford, California
© 1998 by the Board of Trustees of the
Leland Stanford Junior University

Printed in the United States of America

CIP data are at the end of the book

For David Wills

Contents

An oral version of this text, shorter and often different in form, was presented at a colloquium organized by Patrick Mensah and David Wills, hosted by Edouard Glissant, and held on April 23–25, 1992, at the Louisiana State University, Baton Rouge.

This conference, entitled "Echoes from Elsewhere" / "*Renvois d'ailleurs*," was international and bilingual. We were required to deal with problems of *francophonie* outside France, problems of linguistics or literature, politics or culture.

An earlier outline of this paper had already been read at a colloquium organized at the Sorbonne by the International College of Philosophy, under the direction of Christine Buci-Glucksmann.

"Lack" does not reside in the ignorance [*méconnaissance*] of a language (the French language), but in the non-mastery (be it in Creole or French) of an appropriated language. The authoritarian and prestigious intervention of the French language only strengthens the processes [*les processus*] of lack.

The demand of this appropriated language is therefore mediated by a critical revision of the French language. . . .

To the extent that French linguistic hegemony [*le domesticage par la langue française*] is exercised through a mechanism of "humanism," this revision could partake in what might be called an "anti-humanism."

Edouard Glissant, Le Discours antillais

There, a birth to language, through a labyrinthine maze of names and identities coiling up, one around the other: a nostalgic ring of the unique. . . . In this story, I deeply believe that language itself was jealous.

Abdelkebir Khatibi, Amour bilingue

1

—Picture this, imagine someone who would cultivate the French language.

What is called the French language.

Someone whom the French language would cultivate.

And who, as a French citizen, would be, moreover, a subject of French culture, as we say.

Now suppose, for example, that one day this subject of French culture were to tell you in good French:

"I only have one language; it is not mine."

Or rather, and better still:

I am monolingual. My monolingualism dwells, and I call it my dwelling; it feels like one to me, and I remain in it and inhabit it. It inhabits me. The monolingualism in which I draw my very breath is, for me, my element. Not a natural element, not the transparency of the ether, but an absolute habitat. It is impassable, *indisputable*: I cannot challenge it except by testifying to its omnipresence in me. It would always have preceded me. It is me. For me, this monolingualism is me. That certainly does not mean to say, and do not believe, that I am some allegorical figure of this animal or that truth called monolingualism. But I would not be myself outside it. It constitutes me, it dictates even the ipseity of all things to me, and also prescribes a monastic solitude for me; as if, even before learning to speak, I had been bound by some

vows. This inexhaustible solipsism is myself before me. Lastingly.
[*A demeure.*]

Yet it will never be mine, this language, the only one I am
thus destined to speak, as long as speech is possible for me in
life and in death; you see, never will this language be mine. And,
truth to tell, it never was.

You at once appreciate the source of my sufferings, the place
of my passions, my desires, my prayers, the vocation of my hopes,
since this language runs right across them all. But I am wrong,
wrong to speak of a crossing and a place. For it is *on the shores* of
the French language, uniquely, and neither inside nor outside it,
on the unplaceable line of its coast that, since forever, and lastingly [*à demeure*], I wonder if one can love, enjoy oneself [*jouir*],
pray, die from pain, or just die, plain and simple, in another language or without telling anyone about it, without even speaking
at all.

But above all, and this is the double edge of a sharp sword
that I wished to confide to you almost without saying a word: I
suffer and take pleasure in [*jouis de*] what I am telling you in our
aforementioned common language:

"*Yes, I only have one language, yet it is not mine.*"

—You speak the impossible. Your speech does not hold water.
It will always remain incoherent, "inconsistent," as one would say
in English. Apparently inconsistent, at any rate gratuitous in its
phenomenal eloquence, because its rhetoric does the impossible
with meaning. Your statement makes no sense, it has no common
sense, you can see it getting carried away with itself. How could
anyone have a language that is not theirs? Especially if one claims,
as you insist, to have just one, one only, all alone? You are putting
forward a sort of solemn attestation that stupidly drags itself by
the heels into a logical contradiction. A scholar would perhaps

diagnose something worse in a case so serious, which professes, on its own, to be incurable; on its own, your sentence extirpates itself in a logical contradiction heightened by a *performative* or *pragmatic contradiction*. It is desperate. The performative gesture of the enunciation would in the act prove the opposite of what the testimony claims to declare, namely, a certain truth. "And, truth to tell, it never was [mine]," you dared to say. The one who speaks, the subject of the enunciation, yourself, oh yes, the subject of the French language, is understood as doing the opposite of what he says. It is as if, in one and the same breath, you were lying by confessing the lie. A lie from then on incredible that ruins the credit of your rhetoric. The lie belies itself by virtue of the deed it does [*par le fait de ce qu'il fait*], by the act of language. Thus it proves, practically, the opposite of what your speech intends to assert, prove, and give to be verified. People will not stop denouncing your absurdity.

—Is that so? But then why would they not stop? Why should that last? Even you cannot seem to manage to convince yourself, and you multiply your objection, always making the same one, and exhausting yourself in redundancy.

—The moment you say in French that the French language— the one you are speaking in this manner, here at this very moment, the one which renders our words intelligible, more or less (to whom are we speaking, moreover, and for whom? and shall we ever be translated?)—well, that it is not your language, even though you have no other one, not only will you find yourself caught up in the "performative contradiction" of enunciation, but you will also worsen the logical absurdity, the lie, in fact, or even the perjury within the statement. How could one have only one language without having any, without any which is theirs? Their

very own? And how does one know it? How does one claim to
have any knowledge of it? How does one say it? Why would one
want to have others share this knowledge so long as one is alleg-
ing equally, and in the same outburst of the same idiom, that one
does not know or practice any other language?

— Stop. Do not play that trick on us again, please. To whom
is the reproach of "performative contradiction" often hastily addressed nowadays? To those who are wondering, asking themselves questions, and sometimes making it their duty to tie themselves into knots with it. Certain German or Anglo-American
theorists believe they have discovered an unanswerable strategy
there. They make a specialty of this puerile weapon. At regular
intervals, they are to be found aiming [*poindre*] the same criti-
cism at some adversary or other, preferably a French language
philosopher. Occasionally, some French philosophers also import
this weapon or imprint a national patent upon it when they have
the same enemies, the "enemies within." One could give a good
many examples. This childish armory comprises one single, weak
polemical device. Its mechanism amounts roughly to this: "Ah!
So you ask yourself questions about truth. Well, to that very extent, you do not as yet believe in truth; you are contesting the
possibility of truth. That being the case, how do you expect your
statements to be taken seriously when they lay a claim to some
truth, beginning with your so-called questions? What you are
saying is not true because you are questioning truth. Come on!
you are a skeptic, a relativist, a nihilist; you are not a serious philosopher! If you continue, you will be placed in a department of
rhetoric or literature. If you push the matter further, the condem-
nation or exile could be more serious. You will be confined to the
department of sophistry because what you are doing actually falls
within the province of sophism; it is never far from lying, "perjury," and false evidence. You do not believe what you are saying;

you want to mislead us. And now in order to stir us and win us to your cause, there you are, playing the card of the exile and im-migrant worker, there you are, claiming, in French, that French has always been a foreign language to you! Come off it! If that were true, you would not even know how to say it; you would not know how to say it so well!

(I draw your attention to a first slippage: up until now, I have never spoken of a "foreign language."

When I said that the only language I speak is *not mine*, I did not say it was foreign to me. There is a difference. It is not entirely the same thing, we shall come to it.)

That this scene is as old as the world—at any rate, as old as philosophy—does not bother the prosecutors. We will conclude euphemistically that they have a short memory. They are out of training.

Let us not revive this debate today. My mind is elsewhere, and even if I had not attempted to respond, and so often, to this type of objection, that would not prevent me at this instant from installing myself resolutely, with all the requisite imprudence, within the provocation of that so-called "performative contradic-tion," at this very instant when the phrase has become envenomed with perjury and logical incompatibility. Nothing will prevent me from repeating to whoever wants to hear it—and from signing this public declaration:

"It is possible to be monolingual (I thoroughly am, aren't I?) and speak a language that is not one's own."

—That remains for you to demonstrate.

—Yes, indeed.

—In order to demonstrate something, it is first of all necessary to understand what one wants to demonstrate, what one means or what one wants to mean, what you dare claim to mean where for such a long time, according to you, it would be necessary to think a thought that has no meaning.

—Yes, indeed. But grant me then that "to demonstrate" will also mean something else, and it is this something else, this other meaning, this other scene of demonstration, that is important to me.

—I am listening. What is the meaning of this attestation you are claiming to sign?

2

—Well, before beginning, I will first risk two propositions. They will also appear incompossible. Not only contradictory *in themselves*, this time, but also contradictory *between themselves*. They each take the form of a law. You will call the relationship of antagonism that these two laws maintain each time between themselves an *antinomy*, if you like that word of which I am fond.

—Very well. So what might these two propositions be? I am listening.

—Here they are:

1. *We only ever speak one language.*
2. *We never speak only one language.*

The second proposition approaches the meaning of what my friend Khatibi clearly sets forth in the Introduction to a work on bilingualism, at the moment of defining in sum [*en somme*] a *problematic* and a *program*. I therefore call him to my aid:

If (as we are saying along with others, and after them) there is no such thing as *the* language, if there is no such thing as absolute monolingualism, one still has to define what a mother tongue is in its active division, and what is transplanted between this language and the one called foreign. What is transplanted and lost there, belonging neither to the one nor the other: the incommunicable.

Of bi-language, in its effects of speech and writing.[1]

"Division," he says. "Active division." That, perhaps, is why one writes and how one dreams of writing. And that is why there are two motivations instead of one, a single reason but a reason wrought by the said "division," that is why in always doing that one recollects, one troubles oneself, one goes in search of history and filiation. In this place of jealousy, in this place that is divided between vengeance and resentment [*ressentiment*], in this body fascinated by its own "division," before any other memory, writing destines itself, as if acting on its own, to anamnesia.

Even if it forgets it, writing still summons this memory, it summons itself in this way, it summons itself from memory. A blind genealogical impulse would find its moving source, its force, and its recourse in the very partition of this double law, in the antinomical duplicity of this clause of belonging:

1. *We only ever speak one language — or rather one idiom only.*
2. *We never speak only one language — or rather there is no pure idiom.*

— So would that be possible? You are asking me to take your word for it. And you have just added "idiom" to "language." That changes many things. A language is no idiom, nor is the idiom a dialect.

— I'm not unaware of the necessity of these distinctions. Linguists and scholars in general can have good reasons for upholding them. Nevertheless, in all rigor, and stretched to their extreme limit, I do not believe them to be tenable. If we do not take into consideration, in an always very determined context, some *external* criteria, whether they are "quantitative" (the age, stability, and demographic extension of the field of speech) or "politico-symbolic" (the legitimacy, authority, and domination of a language over a speech, dialect, or idiom), then I do not know where we can find *internal* and *structural* features in order to distinguish rigorously between a language, a dialect, and an idiom.

At any rate, even if what I am saying there remains problematic, I would still position myself at this viewpoint, from which, provisionally, and at least by agreement [*convention*] between us, that distinction is still suspended. For the phenomena that interest me are precisely those that blur these boundaries, cross them, and make their historical artifice appear, also their violence, meaning the relations of force that are concentrated there and actually capitalize themselves there interminably. Those who are sensitive to all the stakes of "creolization," for example, assess this better than others.

—I do accept the proposed agreement, and since you want to narrate your story, give testimony in your name, speak of what is "yours" and what is not, it remains for me, one more time, to take your word for it.

—Is that not what we always do when someone is speaking, and hence attesting? And yes, I too believe in this antinomy, it is possible and that is what I think I know. From experience, as we say, and that is what I would like to demonstrate, or, rather than demonstrating it "logically," to restage and recall it as the "cause of effects" [*raison des effets*]. And rather than recalling, to remind *myself*. Myself. To remind myself, to myself as myself.

What I would like to remind myself of, that to which I would like to recall myself, are the intractable traits [*traits intraitables*] of an impossibility, an impossibility so impossible and intractable that it is not far from calling an interdiction to mind. There would be a necessity in that, but the necessity of what presents itself as impossible-forbidden ("You cannot do that! Of course not!—But of course yes!—Of course not; if I were you I would not do it!—But of course yes; if you were me, you would do that, nothing but that!—Of course not!")—and a necessity that, however, is there and that works: translation, a translation other than the one spoken about by convention, common sense, and certain doctrinaires of translation. For this double postulation,

— *We only ever speak one language . . .*
      (yes, but)
— *We never speak only one language . . .*

is not only the very law of what is called translation. It would also be the law itself as translation. A law which is a little mad, I am willing to grant you that. But you see, that is not very original, and, later on, I shall repeat it again: I have always suspected the law, as well as language, of being mad, of being, at any rate, the unique place and the first condition of madness.

So this meeting—which had just opened, as you recall—was an international colloquium. In Louisiana, which is not, as you know, anywhere in France. Generous hospitality. Invited guests? Francophones *belonging*, as we strangely say, to several nations, cultures, and states. And all these problems of *identity*, as we so foolishly say nowadays. Among all the participants, there were two, Abdelkebir Khatibi and myself, who, besides an old friendship, meaning the blessing of so many other things from memory and the heart, also shared a certain destiny. They live in a certain "state" as far as language and culture are concerned: they have a certain status.

In what is so named and is indeed "my country," this status is given the title of "Franco-Maghrebian" [*Franco-Maghrébin*].

What can that possibly mean to say, I ask you, you who are fond of meaning-to-say [*vouloir-dire*]? What is the nature of that hyphen? What does it want? What is Franco-Maghrebian? *Who* is a "Franco-Maghrebian"?

In order to know *who* a Franco-Maghrebian is, it is necessary to know *what Franco-Maghrebian is*, what "Franco-Maghrebian" means. To put it the other way round, by inverting the circulation of the circle in order to determine, *vice versa, what it is to be Franco-Maghrebian*, it would be necessary to know who is, and (Oh Aristotle!) above all who is the *most* Franco-Maghrebian. As a model, let us use a logic that would be, say, of the Aristotelian type: we model ourselves upon what *is* "most this or that" or what *is* "the best this or that," for example, upon the entity [*l'étant*] par excellence in order to reach down to thinking the being of what is *in general*, proceeding that way regarding the being of the entity [*l'être de l'étant*], from theology to ontology and not the reverse (even if actually things are, as you will say, more complicated, but that is not the subject).

According to a circular law with which philosophy is familiar, we will affirm then that the one who is *most*, most purely, or most rigorously, most essentially, Franco-Maghrebian would allow us to decipher *what it is to be* Franco-Maghrebian *in general*. We will decipher the essence of the Franco-Maghrebian from the paradigmatic example of the "*most* Franco-Maghrebian," the Franco-Maghrebian par excellence.

Still, assuming there were some historical unity of *a* France and *a* Maghreb, which is far from being certain, the "and" will never have been given, only promised or claimed. At bottom, that is what we must be talking about, what we are talking about without fail, even if we are doing it by omission. The silence of that hyphen does not pacify or appease anything, not a single torment, not a single torture. It will never silence their memory. It could even worsen the terror, the lesions, and the wounds. A hyphen is never enough to conceal protests, cries of anger or suffering, the noise of weapons, airplanes, and bombs.

3

So let us form a hypothesis, and leave it to work. Let us suppose that without wishing to hurt Abdelkebir Khatibi's feelings, one day at the colloquium in Louisiana, far from his home and from mine, also far from our home, I make him a declaration through the loyal and admiring affection I feel for him. What would this public declaration declare to him? Approximately the following: "You see, dear Abdelkebir, between the two of us, I consider myself to be the *most* Franco-Maghrebian, and perhaps even the *only* Franco-Maghrebian here. If I am mistaken, in error, or being misleading, then, well, I am certain someone will contradict me. I would then attempt to explain or justify myself in the best way I can. Let us look around us and classify, separate, and take things one group at a time.

"A. Among us, there are Francophone French speakers who are not Maghrebian: French speakers from France, in a word, French citizens who have come here from France.

"B. There are also among us some 'Francophones' who are neither French nor Maghrebian: Swiss, Canadians, Belgians, or Africans from various Central African countries.

"C. Finally, among us there are French-speaking Maghrebians who are not and have never been French, meaning French citizens: yourself, for example, and other Moroccans or Tunisians.

"Now, as you can see, I do not belong to any of these clearly defined groups. My 'identity' does not fall under any of these three categories. Where would I categorize myself then? What taxonomy should I invent?

"My hypothesis is, therefore, that I am perhaps the *only* one here who can call himself at once a Maghrebian (which is not a citizenship) and a French citizen. One and the other at the same time. And better yet, at once one and the other *by birth*. Birth, nationality by birth, native culture—is that not our theme here? (One day it will be necessary to devote another colloquium to language, nationality, and cultural belonging, *by death* this time around, by sepulture, and to begin with the secret of Oedipus at Colonus: all the power that this 'alien' holds over 'aliens' in the innermost secret place of the secret of his last resting place, a secret that he guards, or confides to the guardianship of Theseus in exchange for the salvation of the city and generations to come, a secret that, nevertheless, he refuses to his daughters, while depriving them of even their tears, and a just 'work of mourning.')

"Did we not agree to speak here of the language called maternal, about birth as it relates to soil, birth as it relates to blood, and birth as it relates to language, which means something entirely other? And about the relationships between birth, language, culture, nationality, and citizenship?

"That my 'case' does not fall under any of the three groups that were represented at that time, such was, at least, my hypothesis. Was that not also the only justification, if there was one, for my presence at this colloquium?"

That, roughly, is what I would have begun by declaring to Abdelkebir Khatibi.

What you want to listen to at this moment is the story that I tell myself, the one that I would like to tell myself, or that, perhaps on account of the sign, writing, and anamnesia, and also in response to the title of that meeting, the title *Renvois d'ailleurs* or *Echoes from Elsewhere*, I am limiting, without a doubt, to a little fable.

If I have indeed revealed the sentiment of being the only Franco-Maghrebian here or there, that does not authorize me to speak in the name of anyone, especially not about some Franco-Maghrebian entity whose identity remains in question. We will come back to that, for all of that is, in my case, far from being so clear.

Our question is still identity. What is identity, this concept of which the transparent identity to itself is always dogmatically presupposed by so many debates on monoculturalism or multi-culturalism, nationality, citizenship, and, in general, belonging? And before the identity of the subject, what is *ipseity*? The latter is not reducible to an abstract capacity to say "I," which it will always have preceded. Perhaps it signifies, in the first place, the power of an "I can," which is more originary than the "I" in a chain where the "*pse*" of *ipse* no longer allows itself to be dissociated from power, from the mastery and sovereignty of the *hospes* (here, I am referring to the semantic chain that works on the body of hospitality as well as hostility—*hostis, hospes, hosti-pet, posis, despotes, potere, potis sum, possum, pote est, potest, pot sedere, possidere, compos,* etc.—)[2]

To be a Franco-Maghrebian, one "like myself," is not, not particularly, and particularly not, a surfeit or richness of identities, attributes, or names. In the first place, it would rather betray a *disorder of identity* [*trouble d'identité*].

Recognize in that expression "disorder of identity" all its seriousness without excluding its psychopathological or socio-pathological connotations. In order to present myself as a Franco-Maghrebian, I made an allusion to *citizenship*. As we know, citizenship does not define a cultural, linguistic, or, in general, historical participation. It does not cover all these modes of belonging. But it is not some superficial or superstructural predicate floating on the surface of experience.

Especially not when this citizenship is, through and through, *precarious, recent, threatened,* and more artificial than ever. That is "my case"; the at once typical and uncommon situation of which I would like to speak. Especially not when one has obtained this citizenship in the course of one's life, which has perhaps happened to several Americans present at this colloquium, but also, and above all, not when one has lost it *in the course of one's life,* which has certainly not happened to almost any American. And if one day some individual or other has seen their citizenship *itself* withdrawn (which is more than a passport, a "green card," an eligibility or right to vote), has that ever happened to a *group* as such? I am of course not referring to some ethnic group seceding, liberating itself one day, from another nation-state, or giving up one citizenship in order to give itself another one in a newly instituted state. There are too many examples of this mutation.

No, I am speaking of a "community" group (a "mass" assembling together tens or hundreds of thousands of persons), a supposedly "ethnic" or "religious" group that finds itself one day deprived, as a group, of its citizenship by a state that, with the brutality of a unilateral decision, withdraws it without asking for their opinion, and *without the said group gaining back any other citizenship. No other.*

Now I have experienced that. Along with others, I lost and then gained back French citizenship. I lost it for years without having another. You see, not a single one. I did not ask for anything. I hardly knew, at the time, that it had been taken away from me, not, at any rate, in the legal and objective form of knowledge in which I am explaining it here (for, alas, I got to know it in another way). And then, one day, one "fine day," without, once again, my asking for anything, and still too young to know it in a properly political way, I found the aforementioned citizenship again. The state, to which I never spoke, had given it back to me. The state, which was no longer Pétain's "French State," was recognizing me anew. That was, I think, in 1943; I had still never gone "to France"; I had never been there.

In essence, a citizenship does not sprout up just like that. It is not natural. But, as in the flash of a privileged revelation, the artifice and precariousness of citizenship appear better when it is inscribed in memory as a recent acquisition: for example, the French citizenship granted to the Jews of Algeria by the Crémieux decree in 1870. Or, better yet, in the traumatic memory of a "degradation," of a loss of citizenship: for example, the loss of French citizenship, less than a century later, for the same Jews of Algeria.

Such was, indeed, the case "under the Occupation," as we say.

Yes, "as we say," for it is actually a legend. Algeria has never been occupied. I mean that if it has ever been occupied, the German Occupant was never responsible for it. The withdrawal of French citizenship from the Jews of Algeria, with everything that followed, was the deed of the French alone. They decided that all by themselves, in their heads; they must have been dreaming about it all along; they implemented it all by themselves.

I was very young at that time, and I certainly did not understand very well—already, I did not understand very well—what citizenship and loss of citizenship *meant to say*. But I do not doubt that exclusion—from the school reserved for young French citizens—could have a relationship to the disorder of identity of which I was speaking to you a moment ago. I do not doubt either that such "exclusions" come to leave their mark upon this belonging or non-belonging *of* language, this affiliation *to* language, this assignation to what is peacefully called a language.

But who exactly possesses it? And whom does it possess? Is language in possession, ever a possessing or possessed possession? Possessed or possessing in exclusive possession, like a piece of personal property? What of this being-at-home [*être-chez-soi*] in language toward which we never cease returning?

I have just emphasized that the ablation of citizenship lasted for two years, but it did not, *strictu sensu*, occur "under the Occupation." It was a Franco-French operation, one even ought to say an act of French Algeria in the absence of any German occupation. One never saw a German uniform in Algeria. No alibi, denial, or illusion is possible: it was impossible to transfer the responsibility of that exclusion upon an occupying alien.

We were hostages of the French, enduringly [*à demeure*]; something of it remains with me, no matter how much I travel.

And I repeat it: I do not know whether there are other examples of this in the history of modern nation-states, examples of such a deprivation of citizenship decreed for tens and tens of thousands of people at a time. In October 1940, by abolishing the Crémieux decree of October 24, 1870, France herself, the French state in Algeria, the "French state" legally constituted (by the Chamber of the Popular Front!) following the well-known act of parliament, this state was refusing French identity to—rather, taking it away again from—those whose collective memory continued to recollect or had barely just forgotten that it had been lent to them as if only the day before and had not failed to give rise, less than half a century earlier (1898), to murderous persecutions and the beginnings of pogroms. Without, however, preventing an unprecedented "assimilation": profound, rapid, zealous, and spectacular. In two generations.

Does this "disorder of identity" favor or inhibit anamnesia?

Does it heighten the desire of memory, or does it drive the gene-alogical fantasy to despair? Does it suppress, repress, or liberate? All of these at the same time, no doubt, and that would be another version, the other side of the contradiction that set us in motion. And has us running to the point of losing our breath, or our minds.

4

Under this heading, the monolingualism of the other, let us exercise our imagination. Let us sketch out a figure. It will have only a vague *resemblance* to myself and to the kind of auto-biographical anamnesis that always appears like the thing to do when one exposes oneself in the space of *relation*. Let us understand "relation" in the sense of narration, the narration of the genealogical narrative, for example, but more generally as well, in the sense that Edouard Glissant imprints upon the expression when he speaks of *Poetics of Relation* [*Poétique de la Relation*], just as one could also speak of a politics of relation.

I therefore venture to present myself to you here, *ecce homo*, in parody, as the exemplary Franco-Maghrebian, but disarmed, with accents that are more naïve, less controlled, and less polished. *Ecce homo*, and do not smile, for a "passion" would indeed appear to be at stake here, the martyrdom of the Franco-Maghrebian who from birth, since his birth but also from his birth on the other coast, his coast, has, at bottom, chosen and understood nothing, and who still suffers and testifies.

As regards so enigmatic a value as that of attestation, or even of exemplarity in testimony, here is a first question, the most general one, without the shadow of a doubt. What happens when someone resorts to describing an allegedly uncommon "situation," mine, for example, by testifying to it in terms that go beyond it, in a language whose generality takes on a value that is in some way structural, universal, transcendental, or ontological? When anybody who happens by infers the following: "What holds for me, irreplaceably, also applies to all. Substitution is in progress; it has already taken effect. Everyone can say the same thing for themselves and of themselves. It suffices to hear me; I am the universal hostage."

How does one describe this time, then; how does one designate this unique time? How does one determine this, an uncommon this whose uniqueness stems from testimony alone, from the fact that certain individuals in certain situations testify to the features of a structure nevertheless universal, revealing it, showing it, and allowing it to be read "more vividly," more vividly as one says, and because, above all, one says it about an injury, more vividly and *better than others*, and sometimes alone in their category? And what makes it more unbelievable is that they are alone in a genre which becomes in turn a universal example, thus interbreeding and accumulating the two logics, that of exemplarity and that of the host as hostage.

—That is not what surprises me most. For one can *testify* only to the unbelievable. To what can, at any rate, only be believed; to what appeals only to belief and hence to the given word, since it lies beyond the limits of proof, indication, certified acknowledgment [*le constat*], and knowledge. Whether we like it or not, and whether we know it or not, when we ask others to take our word for it, we are already in the order of what is merely believable. It is always a matter of what is offered to faith and of appealing to faith, a matter of what is only "believable" and hence as unbelievable as a miracle. Unbelievable because *merely* "credible." The order of attestation itself testifies to the miraculous, to the unbelievable believable: to what must be believed all the same, whether believable or not. Such is the truth to which I am appealing, and which must be believed, even, and especially, when I am lying or betraying my oath. Even in false testimony, this truth presupposes veracity — and not the reverse.

— Yes, and as I was saying, what makes it more unbelievable is that such individuals testify this way in a language they speak, of course, one that they agree to speak in a certain way and up to a certain point . . .

— . . . in a certain way and up to a certain point, as one ought to say about any practice of language . . .

— . . . but one which they speak by presenting it, *in that very language, as the language of the other*. Such will have been, this time, the experience of the majority of us when we were speaking English at that meeting. But how would I do it, on this very spot, by speaking to you in French? By what right?

Here is an example. What did I do a short while ago by uttering a maxim such as "I have only one language, yet it is not mine," or "we only ever speak one language"? What did I wish to do by continuing in approximately the following manner: "Therefore there is no such thing as bilingualism or plurilingualism"? Or still, and multiplying the contradictions in this manner, "We never speak only one language," therefore, "There is nothing but plurilingualism"? So many apparently contradictory assertions (there is no such thing as *x*, there is nothing but *x*), so many claims of which I indeed believe, however, that, given the time, I would be capable of demonstrating the universal value. Anyone should be able to say "I only have one language (yet, but, henceforth, lastingly [*à demeure*]) it is not mine."

An immanent structure of promise or desire, an expectation without a horizon of expectation, informs all speech. As soon as I speak, before even formulating a promise, an expectation, or a desire *as such*, and when I still do not know what will happen to me or what awaits me at the end of a sentence, neither *who* nor *what* awaits whom or what, I am within this promise or this threat—which, from then on, gathers the language together, the promised or threatened language, promising all the way to the point of threatening and *vice versa*, thus gathered together in its very dissemination. Since subjects competent in several languages *tend* to speak only one language, even where the latter is dismembering itself, and because it can only promise and promise itself by threatening to dismember itself, a language can only speak itself of itself. One cannot speak of a language except in that language. Even if to place it outside itself.

Far from sealing off anything, this solipsism conditions the address to the other, it gives its word, or rather it gives the possibility of giving its word, it gives the given word in the ordeal of a threatening and threatened promise:[3] monolingualism and tautology, the absolute impossibility of metalanguage. The impossibility of an absolute metalanguage, at least, for some *effects* of metalanguage, effects or relative phenomena, namely, relays of metalanguage "within" a language, already introduce into it some translation and some objectification in progress. At the horizon, visible and miraculous, spectral but infinitely desirable, they allow the mirage of another language to tremble.

—What I am having some difficulty understanding is this entire vocabulary of having, habit, and possession of a language that would or would not be one's own—yours, for example. As if the possessive pronoun and adjective were, as far as language goes, proscribed here by language.

—On the part of one who speaks or writes the aforementioned language, this experience of monolingual solipsism is never one of belonging, property, power of mastery, pure "ipseity" (hospitality or hostility) of whichever kind. Though the "non-mastery . . . of an appropriated language" of which Glissant speaks qualifies, above all, more literally and more sensitively, some situations of "colonial" alienation or historical servitude, this definition, so long as it is imprinted with the requisite inflections, also carries well beyond these determinate conditions. It also holds for what would be called the language of the master, the *hospes*, or the colonist.

Quite far from dissolving the always relative specificity, however cruel, of situations of linguistic oppression or colonial expropriation, this prudent and differentiated universalization must account, and I would even say that it is the only way one can account, for the *determinable* possibility of a subservience and a hegemony. And even account for a terror inside languages (inside languages there is a terror, soft, discreet, or glaring; that is our subject). For contrary to what one is often most tempted to believe, the master is nothing. And he does not have exclusive possession of anything. Because the master does not possess exclusively, and *naturally*, what he calls his language, because, whatever he wants or does, he cannot maintain any relations of property or identity that are natural, national, congenital, or ontological, with it, because he can give substance to and articulate [*dire*] this appropriation only in the course of an unnatural process of politico-phantasmatic constructions, because language is not his natural possession, he can, thanks to that very fact, pretend historically, through the rape of a cultural usurpation, which means always essentially colonial, to appropriate it in order to impose it as "his own." That is his belief; he wishes to make others share it through the use of force or cunning; he wants to make others believe it, as they do a miracle, through rhetoric, the school, or the army. It suffices for him, through whatever means there is, to make himself understood, to have his "speech act" work, to create conditions for that, in order that he may be "happy" ("felicitous"—which means, in this code, efficacious, productive, efficient, generative of the expected event, but sometimes anything but "happy") and the trick is played, a *first trick* will have, at any rate, been played.

Liberation, emancipation, and revolution will necessarily be the second trick. It will provide freedom from the first while confirming a heritage by internalizing it, by reappropriating it—but only up to a certain point, for, as my hypothesis shows, there is never any such thing as absolute appropriation or reappropriation. Because there is no natural property of language, language gives rise only to appropriative madness, to jealousy without appropriation. Language speaks this jealousy; it is nothing but jealousy unleashed. It takes its revenge at the heart of the law. The law that, moreover, language itself is, apart from also being mad. Mad about itself. Raving mad.

(As this goes without saying and does not deserve any overly long development here, let us recall briefly, in passing, that this discourse on the ex-appropriation of language, more precisely, of the "mark," opens out onto a politics, a right, and an ethics: let us even go so far as to say that it is the only one with the power to do it, whatever the risks are, precisely because the undecidable ambiguity runs those risks and therefore appeals to the decision where it conditions, prior to any program and even any axiomatics, the right and the limits of a right to property, a right to hospitality, a right to *ipseity* in general, to the "power" of the *hospes* himself, the master and possessor, particularly of himself—*ipse, compos, ipsissimus, despotes, potior, possidere*, to cite in no particular order a chain reconstructed by Benveniste of which we were speaking earlier.)

So much so that "colonialism" and "colonization" are only high points [*reliefs*], one traumatism over another, an increasing buildup of violence, the jealous rage of an essential *coloniality* and *culture*, as shown by the two names. A coloniality of culture, and, without a doubt, also of hospitality when the latter conditions and auto-limits itself into a law, however "cosmopolitan"— as the Kant of perpetual peace and universal right wanted.

Consequently, anyone should be able to declare under oath: I have only one language and it is not mine; my "own" language is, for me, a language that cannot be assimilated. My language, the only one I hear myself speak and agree to speak, is the language of the other.

This abiding "alienation" [*aliénation à demeure*] appears, like "lack," to be constitutive. But it is neither a lack nor an alienation; it lacks nothing that precedes or follows it, it alienates no *ipseity*, no property, and no self that has ever been able to represent its watchful eye. Although this injunction issues a summons, lastingly [*mette en demeure à demeure*],[4] nothing else "is there" ever to watch over its past or future. This structure of alienation without alienation, this inalienable alienation, is not only the origin of our responsibility, it also structures the peculiarity [*le propre*] and property of language. It institutes the *phenomenon* of hearing-oneself-speak in order to mean-to-say [*pour vouloir dire*]. But here, we must say the *phenomenon* as *phantasm*. Let us refer for the moment to the semantic and etymological affinity that associates the phantasm to the *phainesthai*, to phenomenality, but also to the spectrality of the phenomenon. *Phantasma* is also the phantom, the double, or the ghost. We are there.

—Do you mean we belong among them?

—Who, upon reading and understanding us properly, here . . .

—Here?

—. . . or there, will dare to have someone believe the opposite? Who would dare claim to prove it? Being here in an element of which the spectral phantasmaticity cannot, under any circumstances, be reduced does not imply that political and historical terror is alleviated on that account, quite the contrary. For there are situations, experiences, and subjects who are, precisely, in a *situation* (but what does *situating* mean in this case?) to testify exemplarily to them. This exemplarity is no longer reducible to that of an example in a series . . . Rather, it would be the exemplarity—remarkable and remarking—that allows one to read in a more dazzling, intense, or even *traumatic* manner the truth of a universal necessity. The structure appears in the experience of the injury, the offense, vengeance, and the lesion. In the experience of terror. It is a traumatic event because at stake here are blows and injuries, scars, often murders, and sometimes collective assassinations. It is reality itself, the scope [*portée*] of any *férance*, of any reference as différance.

That being the case, what status must be assigned to this exemplarity of re-mark? How do we interpret the history of an example that allows the re-inscription of the structure of a universal law upon the body of an irreplaceable singularity in order to render it thus remarkable?

Already, this is an abyssal problem that we cannot treat here in its classical form. Even so, one must, still from the abyss, take note of a chance that is bound to complicate the deal or the folding, and involve the fold in dissemination, *as* dissemination. For it is in the form of a thinking of the unique, precisely, and not of the plural, as it was too often believed, that a thought of dissemination formerly introduced itself as a folding thought of the fold—and as a folded thought of the fold.[5] Because the fold of such a *re-mark* is there, the replica or re-application of the quasi-transcendental or quasi-ontological within the phenomenal, ontical, or empirical example, and within the phantasm itself where the latter presupposes the trace in language, we are justifiably obliged to say at once that "we only ever speak one language," and "we never speak only one language" or "I only speak one language, (and, but, yet) it is not mine."

For is the experience of language (or rather, before any discourse, the experience of the mark, the re-mark or the margin) not precisely what makes this *articulation* possible and necessary? Is that not what *gives rise* to this articulation between transcendental or ontological universality, and the exemplary or testimonial singularity of *martyred* existence? While evoking apparently abstract notions of the mark or the re-mark here, we are also thinking of scars. Terror is practiced at the expense of wounds inscribed on the body. We speak here of martyrdom and passion in the strict and quasi-etymological sense of these terms. And when we mention the body, we are naming the body of language and writing, as well as what makes them a thing of the body. We therefore appeal to what is, so hastily, named the body proper, which happens to be affected by the same ex-appropriation, the same "alienation" without alienation, without any property that is forever lost or to be ever reappropriated.

Do you hear this word, *jamais*, in our language? And what about *sans*? Do you hear without ever understanding? That is what must, henceforth, be demonstrated in the scene thus created.

In what respect, therefore, can the passion of a Franco-Maghrebian martyr testify to this universal destiny which assigns us to a single language while prohibiting us from appropriating it, given that such an interdiction is linked to the very essence of language, or rather writing, to the very essence of the mark, the fold, and the re-mark?

5

—That is a rather abstract way to narrate a story, this fable you jealously call your story, a story which would be solely yours.

—In its common concept, autobiographical anamnesis presupposes *identification*. And precisely not identity. No, an identity is never given, received, or attained; only the interminable and indefinitely phantasmatic process of identification endures. Whatever the story of a return to oneself or to *one's home* [*chez-soi*], into the "hut" ["case"] of one's home (*chez* is the *casa*), no matter what an odyssey or bildungsroman it might be, in whatever manner one invents the story of a construction of the *self*, the *autos*, or the *ipse*, it is always *imagined* that the one who writes should know how to say *I*. At any rate, the *identificatory modality* must already or henceforth be assured: assured of language and in its language. It is believed that the problem of the unity of language must be resolved, and that the One of language in the strict or broad sense be given—a broad sense that will be stretched till it includes all the models and identificatory modalities, all the poles of imaginary projection in social culture. Each domain is represented there in configuration: politics, religion, the arts, poetry and great literature, literature in the (modern) narrow sense. It is necessary to know already in what language *I* is expressed, and I *am* expressed. Here we are thinking of the *I think*, as well as the grammatical or linguistical *I*, of the *me* [*moi*] or *us* [*nous*] in their identificatory status as it is sculpted by cultural, symbolic, and sociocultural figures. From all viewpoints, which are not just grammatical, logical, or philosophical, it is well known that the *I* of the kind of anamnesis called autobiographical, the I [*je-me*] of *I recall* [*je me rappelle*] is produced and uttered in different ways depending on the language in question. It never precedes them; therefore it is not independent of language in general. That is something well known but rarely taken into consideration by those dealing in general with autobiography—whether this genre is literary or not, whether it is considered, moreover, as a genre or not.

Now without committing ourselves to approach the bottom without bottom of things here, we should perhaps confine ourselves to one sole consequence. It concerns what our common theme [*lieu commun*] was at the colloquium, from its very title, namely, the *ailleurs* ["elsewhere"] and the *renvoi* ["referral"], assuming they could ever give rise to a common theme. We can believe, without the shadow of a doubt, that the *I* in question *formed* itself, if it managed to do at least that, and if the disorder of identity of which we were speaking a while ago does not, precisely, affect the very construction of the *I*, the formation of the *speaking-I* [*dire-je*], the *me-I* [*moi-je*], or the appearance, as such, of a pre-egological ipseity. This *I* would have *formed* itself, then, at the site of a *situation* that cannot be found, a site always referring elsewhere, to something other, to another language, to the other in general. It would have *located* [*situé*] itself in a *nonlocatable* [*insituable*] experience of *language* in the broad sense of the word.

This experience was neither monolingual, nor bilingual, nor plurilingual. It was neither one, nor two, nor two + *n*. At any rate, there was no thinkable or thinking *I* before this strangely familiar and properly improper (uncanny, *unheimlich*) situation of an uncountable language.

What I meant to suggest is that it is impossible to count languages. There is no calculability, since the One of a language, which escapes all arithmetic (ac)countability, is never determined. The One of the monolanguage of which I speak, and the one I speak, will hence not be an arithmetical identity or, in short, any identity at all. Monolanguage remains incalculable, at least in that characteristic. But the fact that languages appear strictly uncountable does not prevent them all from disappearing. In this century they are sinking each day by the hundreds, and this perdition opens the question of another rescue, or another salvation. How do we save a language, a language that is alive and "intact," by doing something other than archiving idioms (which we sometimes do scientifically, if not sufficiently, in a matter of urgency that is becoming more and more pressing)?

What should one think about this new soteriology? Is it good? "Good" in the name of what? What if, in order to save some humans lost in their language, in order to deliver the humans themselves, at the expense of their language, it was better to renounce the language, at least to renounce the best conditions for survival "at all costs" for the idiom? And what if some humans were more worth saving than their language, under circumstances where, alas, one needed to choose between them? For we are living in a period in which the question at times arises. Today, on this earth of humans, certain people must yield to the homo-hegemony of dominant languages. They must learn the language of the masters, of capital and machines; they must lose their idiom in order to survive or live better. A tragic economy, an impossible counsel. I do not know whether salvation for the other presupposes the salvation of the idiom. We will talk about it again, as we would about that strange French word *salut* ["salvation"].

Let us start off again then.

What I am saying, the one I am speaking about, in a word, this *I* of whom I speak is someone to whom, as I more or less recall, access to any non-French language of Algeria (literary or dialectal Arabic, Berber, etc.) was *interdicted*. But this same *I* is also someone to whom access to French was *also interdicted*, in a different, apparently roundabout, and perverted manner. In a different manner, surely, but likewise interdicted. By an interdict that, as a result, interdicted access to the identifications that enable the pacified autobiography, "memoirs" in the classical sense.

In what language does one write memoirs when there has been no authorized mother tongue? How does one utter a worthwhile "I recall" when it is necessary to invent both one's language and one's "I," to invent them *at the same time*, beyond this surging wave of anamnesia that the *double interdict* has unleashed?

—The unleashed, surging wave [*déferlement déchaîné*] of an interdict? What funny language you speak there, once again, indeed . . .

—Yes, an "unleashed, surging wave," for it is suitable here to think of tensions and the play of forces, of the jealous, vindictive, and hidden *physis*, of the generative fury of this repression—and that is why this amnesia remains, in a way, active, dynamic, powerful, something other than a mere forgetfulness. The interdiction is not negative; it does not incite simply to loss. Nor is the amnesia it organizes from the depths, in the nights of the abyss, incited to perdition. It ebbs and flows like a wave that sweeps everything along upon shores that I know too well. It carries everything, that sea, and on two sides; it swells, sweeps along, and enriches itself with everything, carries away, brings back, deports and becomes swollen again with what it has dragged away. The pigheadedness of a capital without a head. Besides I like the French word *déferlement*, and I give my reasons for that elsewhere . . .

It would probably be best for us to avoid lending substance

to familiar categories here and feeling reassured in them, whatever domain they may belong to. We are, for example, giving way to easy complacency and mechanism by speaking of an *interdict*. The interdict—if the name "interdict" is to remain, if we are keen on retaining it—was of a kind at once *exceptional* and *fundamental*. It was engulfing [*déferlant*]. When access to a language is forbidden, nothing—no gesture, no act—is forbidden. One forbids access to speech [*au dire*], that is all, a certain kind of speech. But that is precisely the fundamental interdiction, the absolute interdiction, the interdiction of diction and speech. The interdiction of which I speak, the interdiction from which I tell, tell myself, and tell it to myself, is then not simply one interdiction among others.

Moreover, the name "interdict" still appears too risky. It remains facile and ambiguous to the extent that this limit was never set down, enacted either as an act of law—an official decree, a sentence—or like a physical, natural, or organic barrier. There was neither a natural frontier nor a juridical boundary. We had the choice, the formal right, to learn or not learn Arabic or Berber. Or Hebrew. It was not illegal, or a crime. At the *lycée*, at least— and Arabic rather than Berber. I do not recall anyone ever learning Hebrew at the *lycée*. The interdict worked therefore through other ways. More subtle, peaceful, silent, and liberal ways. It took other forms of revenge. In the manner of permitting and giving, for, in principle, everything was given, or at any rate permitted.

Finally and especially, the experience of this double interdict left no one any recourse. It left *me* none. It could not not be the experience of an overstepping of limits. I am not saying "transgression"—the word is at once too facile and too loaded— but one understands better why I was speaking a while ago about a wave [*déferlement*].

In this overstepping of limits, I would also see a writing [*écriture*], in a certain sense of that word around which I have been lurking for decades. Yes, by this word *écriture* we would indicate, among other things, a certain mode of loving and desperate appropriation of language and through it of a forbidding as well as forbidden speech (for me, the French language was both), and also through it of any forbidden idiom — the loving and jealous vengeance of a new work of training [*dressage*], which attempts to restore the language and believes it is at the same time reinventing it, finally giving it a form (deforming, reforming, and transforming it), making it pay the price of the interdict, or (what no doubt amounts to the same thing) acquitting itself, in its proximity, of the price of the interdict. This gives rise to strange ceremonies, secret and shameful celebrations. Therefore to encrypted operations, to some words under seal circulating in everyone's language.

But how does one orient this writing, this impossible appropriation of the forbidding-forbidden language, this inscription of self in the forbidden language — forbidden for me, to me, but also *by* me (for it can be known that I am, in my own way, a defender of the French language)?

I should rather say: How does one orient the inscription of self *in proximity* to this forbidden language, and not simply in it, in proximity to it, like a complaint lodged next to it, a grievance and, already, an appellant procedure. Such an inscription could not be oriented, in my case, from the space and time of a spoken *mother tongue*, because I had none, precisely, none other than French. I had no language for the *grievance*, a word that I love to hear now in English, in which it signifies, additionally, a complaint without accusation, suffering, and mourning. It would be necessary to think about an almost originary grievance here, because it is not even lamenting a loss: I did not, *to my knowledge*, have anything to lose, other than French, the bereaved [*endeuillée*] language of bereavement. In a grievance like this, one takes on lastingly [*à demeure*] a mourning for what one never had.

For never was I able to call French, this language I am speaking to you, "my mother tongue."

These words do not come to my mouth; they do not come out of my mouth. I leave to others the words "my mother tongue."

That is my culture; it taught me the disasters toward which incantatory invocations of the mother tongue will have pushed humans headlong. My culture was right away a political culture. "My mother tongue" is what they say, what they speak; as for me, I cite and question them. I ask them in their own language, certainly in order to make them understand me, for it is serious, if they indeed know what they are saying and what they are talking about. Especially when, so lightly, they celebrate "fraternity." At bottom, brothers, the mother tongue, and so forth pose the same problem.

It is a bit as if I was dreaming of awakening them to tell them: "Listen, pay attention, now that is enough, you must wake up and leave, otherwise some misfortune will strike you or nothing at all will happen to you, which amounts a bit to the same thing. Except some death. One day, you will see that what you are calling your mother tongue will no longer even respond to you. Off you go, on your way, now. Listen, believe me, do not believe so quickly that you are a people, cease listening without protest to those who say 'listen' . . ."

6

—Abdelkebir Khatibi speaks of his "mother tongue." It is certainly not French, but he speaks about it. He speaks about it in another language. In French, precisely. He makes this little secret public. He publishes his words in our language. In order to say of his mother tongue that—and that is a little personal secret!—it has "lost" him.

—Yes, my friend does not therefore hesitate to say "my mother tongue." He does not speak about it without a trembling that can be heard, without the discreet tremor of language that undersigns the poetic resonance of his entire work. But he does not seem to recoil from the words "mother tongue." That is the confidence I find in this little secret. He even asserts the possessive, which is yet another issue. He dares to. He asserts himself possessively as if no hint of a doubt threatened him here: "My mother tongue," he says.

That settles it [*voilà qui tranche*]. Gently, perhaps, and almost silently, but decisively. The decisiveness of this trait precisely marks the story that I am telling, the tale that I tell myself, the intrigue whose representative I am here, or whose victim, as others will too quickly say. The decisiveness of this trait distinguishes it from the experience described by Khatibi when he listens to the call of writing. Still, one gets the impression of hearing him as he listens to this call at the moment it *resounds*. It reaches him in the form of an echo, it returns to him in the resonance of a bi-language. Khatibi holds the voluble conch of a double language against his ear. But right from the very opening, yes, from the very opening of that remarkable book, *Amour bilingue*, there is a mother. Only one. And what a mother indeed! The one who speaks in the first person raises his voice from the language of his mother. Certainly, he evokes a language of origin which has perhaps "lost" him, but which he himself has not lost. He keeps what has lost him. And naturally, he was also still keeping what he has not lost. As if he could guarantee its salvation, even from his own loss. He had only one mother and, no doubt, more than one mother, but he indeed had *his* mother tongue, a mother tongue, a single mother tongue *plus* another language. He can therefore say "*my* mother tongue," without letting the slightest disturbance appear on the surface:

> Yes, my mother tongue has lost me.
>
> Lost me? But how come? Was I not speaking, writing in my mother tongue with great enjoyment [*jouissance*]? And was bi-language [*bi-langue*] not my chance at exorcism? I mean to say something else. My mother was illiterate. My aunt—my false nanny—was too. A di-glossia at birth which had perhaps destined me for writing, between the book of my god and my foreign language, through secondary birth pangs, beyond any mother, one and unique. As a child, I would call the aunt in place of the mother, the mother in place of the other, always calling for the other, the other."[6]

Although, on one bad day in the last years of her life, my own mother became somewhat aphasic and amnesiac, although at that time she appeared to have forgotten even her name, she was certainly not "illiterate." But as I was suggesting earlier, unlike in the tradition into which Khatibi was born, my mother herself did not, anymore than myself, speak a language that one could call "entirely" maternal.

Let us henceforth attempt to point things out more *directly*, at the risk of misnaming them.

First of all, the interdict. A particular interdict against Arabic or Berber languages was, as I recall, in effect, and let us provisionally retain this word "interdict." For someone from my generation, this took several cultural and social forms. It was first of all something *educational*, something which happens to you "at school," but hardly a measure or decision, rather a pedagogical mechanism [*dispositif pédagogique*]. The interdict originated from an "educational system," as it has been called in France for some time now, without a smile, and without anxiety. Given all the colonial censorships—especially in the urban and suburban milieu where I lived—and given all the social barriers there, the racisms, a now grimacing, now "happy go lucky" xenophobia which was sometimes almost user-friendly or joyful, given the disappearance, then in progress, of Arabic as the official, everyday, administrative language, the one and only option was still the school, and the study of Arabic was restricted to the school, but as an alien language, a strange kind of alien language as the language of the other, but then of course, and this is the strange and troubling part, the other as the nearest neighbor. *Unheimlich.* For me, it was the neighbor's language. For I lived on the edge of an Arab neighborhood, at one of those hidden frontiers [*frontières de nuit*], at once invisible and almost impassable: the segregation there was as efficacious as it was subtle. I have to forgo here the delicate analyses that the social geography of the habitat would call for, as well as the cartography of the primary-school classrooms where there were still little Algerians, Arabs, and Kabyles, who were about to vanish at the door of the lycée. Very near and infinitely far away, such was the distance that experience instilled in us, so to speak. Unforgettable and generalizable.

The *optional* study of Arabic remained, of course. We knew

it was allowed, which meant anything but encouraged. The authority of National Education (of "public education") proposed it for the same reason, at the same time, and in the same form as the study of any foreign language in all the French lycées of Algeria. Arabic, an optional foreign language in Algeria! As if we were being told—and that, in the end, is what we were being told: "Let's see, Latin is required for everyone in sixth grade, of course, not to speak of French, but do you, in addition, want to learn English, or Arabic, or Spanish, or German?" It seems that Berber was never included.

Without having any statistics at my disposal, I remember that the percentage of lycée students who chose Arabic was about zero. Those who, in extremely limited numbers, enrolled in it by a choice that at that time seemed unusual or even bizarre did not even form a homogeneous group. Among them, there were at times students of Algerian origin (the "natives," according to the official appellation), when in exceptional cases, they gained access to the lycée—but not all of them, at that time, turned toward Arabic as a linguistic discipline. Among those who chose Arabic, it seems to me that there were little French Algerians of non-urban origin, children of settlers, who came from the "interior." Following the counsel or desire of their parents, necessity being the law, they thought in advance of the need they would one day have of this language for technical and professional reasons: among other things, in order to make themselves heard, which means also listened to, and obeyed by their agricultural workers. All others, including myself, submitted passively to the interdict. It massively represented the cause, as well as the effect— well, the much sought-after effect—of the growing uselessness, the organized marginalization of those languages, Arabic and Berber. Their weakening [*exténuation*] was calculated by a colonial policy that pretended to treat Algeria as a group of three French departments.

Again, I cannot analyze this politics of language head-on, and I would not like to make too easy use of the world "colonialism." All culture is originarily colonial. In order to recall that, let us not simply rely on etymology. Every culture institutes itself through the unilateral imposition of some "politics" of language. Mastery begins, as we know, through the power of naming, of imposing and legitimating appellations. We know how that went with French in France itself, in revolutionary France as much as, or more than, in monarchical France. This sovereign establishment [*mise en demeure souveraine*] may be open, legal, armed, or cunning, disguised under alibis of "universal" humanism, and sometimes of the most generous hospitality. It always follows or precedes culture like its shadow.

The question here is not to efface the arrogant specificity or the traumatizing brutality of what is called modern colonial war in the "strictest definition" of the expression, at the very moment of military conquest, or when a symbolic conquest prolongs the war by other means. On the contrary. Certain people, myself included, have experienced colonial cruelty from two sides, so to speak. But once again, it reveals the colonial structure of any culture in an exemplary way. It testifies to it in martyrdom, and "vividly" [*en martyre, et "à vif"*].

First and foremost, the monolingualism of the other would be that sovereignty, that law originating from elsewhere, certainly, but also primarily the very language of the Law. And the Law as Language. Its experience would be ostensibly *autonomous*, because I have to speak this law and appropriate it in order to understand it *as if* I was giving it to myself, but it remains necessarily *heteronomous*, for such is, at bottom, the essence of any law. The madness of the law places its possibility lastingly [*à demeure*] inside the dwelling of this auto-heteronomy.

The monolingualism imposed by the other operates by relying upon that foundation, here, through a sovereignty whose essence is always colonial, which tends, repressively and irrepressibly, to reduce language to the One, that is, to the hegemony of the homogeneous. This can be verified everywhere, everywhere this homo-hegemony remains at work in the culture, effacing the folds and flattening the text. To achieve that, colonial power does not need, in its heart of hearts, to organize any spectacular initiatives: religious missions, philanthropic or humanitarian good works, conquest of markets, military expeditions, or genocides.

I will be accused of confusing it all. Of course I am not! But what if, while being attentive to the most rigorous distinctions and respecting the respect of the respectable, we cannot and must not lose sight of this obscure common power, this colonial impulse which will have begun by insinuating itself into, overrunning without delay, what they call, by an expression worn enough to give up the ghost, "the relationship to the other"! or "openness to the other"!

But for this very reason, the monolingualism of the other means another thing, which will be revealed little by little: that in any case we speak only one language—and that we do not *own* it. We only ever speak one language—and, since it returns to the other, it exists asymmetrically, always for *the other*, from the other, kept by the other. Coming from the other, remaining with the other, and returning to the other.

Of course, once access was barred to the language and writing of another—in this case Arabic or Berber—and to all the culture which is inseparable from it as well, the inscription of this limit could not not leave traces. In particular, it had to multiply the symptoms of a fascination in the ostensibly common and privileged practice of French. The elided language—Arabic or Berber, to begin with—certainly became the most alien.

But this privilege did not come without a certain strange and confused proximity. Sometimes I wonder whether this unknown language is not my favorite language. The first of my favorite languages. And like each of my favorite languages (for I confess to having more than one), I especially like to hear it outside of all "communication," in the poetic solemnity of the chant or prayer.

Consequently, it will be all the more difficult for me to show that the French language was also equally forbidden to us. Equally but differently, I admit.

Second, the interdict. I repeat it, this experience is still and especially lived through the school. A history of courses and classes can be seen there, but they are academic courses and classes. Such a phenomenon had to distribute itself according to several areas of generality. It revolved around circles, circles of socio-linguistic enclosure at once eccentric and concentric. For the pupils of the French school in Algeria, whether they were of Algerian origin, "French Nationals,"[7] "French citizens of Algeria," or born in that environment of the Jewish people of Algeria who were at once or successively the one and the other ("indigenous Jews," as one used to say under the Occupation without occupation, indigenous Jews and nevertheless French during a certain period)—for all these groups, French was a language supposed to be maternal, but one whose source, norms, rules, and law were situated elsewhere. We should say they were referred elsewhere in order to evoke or reverse the title of our colloquium. Elsewhere, that means in the Metropole. In the Capital-City-Mother-Fatherland. Sometimes, we would say "France," but mostly "the Metropole," at least in the official language, in the imposed rhetoric of discourses, newspapers, and school. As for my family, and almost always elsewhere, we used to say "France" among ourselves. ("Those people can afford vacations in France"; "that person is going to study in France"; "he is going to take the waters in France, generally at Vichy"; "this teacher is from France"; "this cheese is from France.")

The *metropole*, the Capital-City-Mother-Fatherland, the city of the mother tongue: that was a place which represented, without being it, a faraway country, near but far away, not alien, for that would be too simple, but strange, fantastic, and phantom-like [*fantomal*]. Deep down, I wonder whether one of my first and most imposing figures of spectrality, of spectrality itself, was not France; I mean everything that bore this name (assuming that a country and what bears the name of a country is ever anything else, even for the least suspect of patriots, perhaps for them especially).

A place of fantasy, therefore, at an ungraspable distance. As a model of good speech and good writing, it represented the language of the master. (What's more, I do not think I have ever recognized any other sovereign in my life.) The master took the form, primarily and particularly, of the schoolteacher. The teacher could thus represent, with dignity, the master in general, under the universal features of the good Republic. In an entirely different way than for a French child from France, the Metropole was Elsewhere, at once a strong fortress and an entirely other place. From the irreplaceable placement of this mythical "Overthere," it was necessary to attempt, in vain of course, to measure the infinite distance or the incommensurable proximity of the invisible but radiant hearth from which came to us paradigms of distinction, correctness, elegance, literary or oratory language. The language of the Metropole was the mother tongue; actually, the substitute for a mother tongue (is there ever anything else?) as the language of the other.

For the child from Provence or Brittany, there is surely an analogous phenomenon. Paris can always fill this role of a *metropolis* and occupy that place for a provincial, as the posh districts may do for a certain suburb. Paris is also the capital of Literature. But the other, in this case, no longer has the same transcendence of the *overthere*, the distancing of *being-elsewhere*, the inaccessible authority of a master who lives *overseas*. A sea is lacking there.

For we knew by way of an obscure but certain form of knowledge that Algeria was in no manner of speaking the province, nor Algiers the working-class district. Right from childhood, Algeria was, for us, also a country, and Algiers, a city within a country in a fuzzy sense of this word which coincides neither with the state, nor with the nation, nor with religion, nor even, dare I say, with an authentic community. And in this "country" of Algeria, besides, we were witnessing the reconstitution of the spectral simulacrum of a capital/province structure ("Algiers / the interior," "Algiers/Oran," residential districts generally on hilltops / poor districts often further below).

7

Perhaps we have just described a first circle of generality. Between the model called academic, grammatical, or literary, on the one hand, and spoken language, on the other, *the sea* was there: symbolically an infinite space for all the students of the French school in Algeria, a chasm, an abyss. I did not cross it, body and soul, or body without soul (but will I ever have crossed it, crossed it otherwise?), until, for the first time, sailing across on a boat, on the *Ville d'Alger*, at the age of nineteen. First journey, first crossing of my life, twenty hours of sea-sickness and vomiting—before a week of distress and a child's tears in the sinister boarding house of the "Baz'Grand" (in the *khâgne* of the Louis-le-Grand lycée, in a district I have practically never left since that time).

As some people have already begun to do here and there, we could also "recount" infinitely what was being "recounted" to us about, precisely, the "history of France"; understanding by that what was taught in school under the name of the "history of France": an incredible discipline, a fable and bible, yet a doctrine of indoctrination almost uneffaceable for children of my generation. Without speaking of geography: not a word about Algeria, not a single one concerning its history and its geography, whereas we could draw the coast of Brittany and the Gironde estuary with our eyes closed. And we had to be familiar with them in depth, in bulk, and in detail; indeed, we used to recite by rote the names of the major towns of all the French departments, the smallest tributaries of the Seine, the Rhône, the Loire, or the Garonne, their sources and their mouths. Those four invisible rivers had nearly the allegorical power of the Parisian statues which represent them, and which I discovered much later with great hilarity: I was confronting the truth of my geography lessons. But let that be. I shall content myself with a few allusions to literature. It is the first thing I received from French education in Algeria, the only thing, in any event, that I enjoyed receiving. The discovery of French literature, the access to this so unique mode of writing that is called "French-literature" was the experience of a world without any tangible continuity with the one in which we lived, with almost nothing in common with our natural or social landscapes.

But this discontinuity was forging another one. And it was becoming, as a result, *doubly* revealing. It undoubtedly exhibited the haughtiness that always separates literary culture—"literariness" as a certain treatment of language, meaning, and reference —from non-literary culture, even if this separation is never reducible to the "pure and simple." But outside this essential heterogeneity, outside this universal hierarchy, a brutal severance was, in this particular case, fostering a more acute partition: the one that separates French literature—its history, its works, its models, its cult of the dead, its modes of transmission and celebration, its "posh districts," its names of authors and editors—from the culture "proper" to "French Algerians." One entered French literature only by losing one's accent. I think I have not lost my accent; not everything in my "French Algerian" accent is lost. Its intonation is more apparent in certain "pragmatic" situations (anger or exclamation in familial or familiar surroundings, more often in private than in public, which is a quite reliable criterion for the experience of this strange and precarious distinction). But I would like to hope, I would very much prefer, that no publication permit my "French Algerian" to appear. In the meantime, and until the contrary is proven, I do not believe that anyone can detect *by reading*, if I do not myself declare it, that I am a "French Algerian." I retain, no doubt, a sort of acquired reflex from the necessity of this vigilant transformation. I am not proud of it, I make no doctrine of it, but so it is: an accent—any French accent, but above all a strong southern accent—seems incompatible to me with the intellectual dignity of public speech. (Inadmissible, isn't it? Well, I admit it.) Incompatible, a fortiori, with the vocation of a poetic speech: for example, when I heard René Char read his sententious aphorisms with an accent that struck me as at once comical and obscene, as the betrayal of a truth, it ruined, in no small measure, an admiration of my youth.

The accent indicates a hand-to-hand combat with language in general; it says more than accentuation. Its symptomatology invades writing. That is unjust, but it is so. Throughout the story I am relating, despite everything I sometimes appear to profess, I concede that I have contracted a shameful but intractable intolerance: at least in French, insofar as the language is concerned, I cannot bear or admire anything other than pure French. As I do in all fields, I have never ceased calling into question the motif of "purity" in all its forms (the first impulse of what is called "deconstruction" carries it toward this "critique" of the phantasm or the axiom of purity, or toward the analytical decomposition of a purification that would lead back to the indecomposable simplicity of the origin), I still do not dare admit this compulsive demand for a purity of language except within boundaries of which I can be sure: this demand is neither ethical, political, nor social. It does not inspire any judgment in me. It simply exposes me to suffering when someone, who can be myself, happens to fall short of it. I suffer even further when I catch myself or am caught "red-handed" in the act. (There I go again, speaking about offenses in spite of what I have just disclaimed.) Above all, this demand remains so inflexible that it sometimes goes beyond the grammatical point of view, it even neglects "style" in order to bow to a more hidden rule, to "listen" to the domineering murmur of an order which someone in me flatters himself to understand, even in situations where he would be the only one to do so, in a tête-à-tête with the idiom, the final target: a last will of the language, in sum, a law of the language that would entrust itself only to me. As if I were its last heir, the last defender and illustrator of the French language (from here, I can hear the protests, from various sides: yes, yes, laugh away!). As if I were seeking to play that role, to identify myself with this hero-martyr-pioneer-outlaw-legislator who will not hesitate to show clearly that this last will, in its imperative and categorical purity, does not coincide with anything that is given (the lexicon, grammar, stylistic or poetic decorum)—who would not hesitate therefore to violate all these instructions, to burn everything in order to surrender himself to language, to this language.

For, I confess, I always surrender myself to language.

But to mine as to that of the other, and I surrender to it with the almost always premeditated intention of seeing to it that it cannot return: not from there, not here, and not there, there and not here, not in order to give credit to anything that is given, but only to that which is to come, and that is why I speak of a heritage or of a last will.

I therefore admit to a purity which is not very pure. Anything but purism. It is, at least, the only impure "purity" for which I dare confess a taste. It is a pronounced taste for a certain pronunciation. I have never ceased learning, especially when teaching, to speak softly, a difficult task for a "pied noir," and especially from within my family, but to ensure that this soft-spokenness reveal the reserve of what is thus held in reserve, with difficulty, and with great difficulty, contained by the floodgate, a precarious floodgate that allows one to apprehend the catastrophe. The worst can happen at every turn.

I say "floodgate," a floodgate of the verb and of the voice. I have spoken a great deal about this elsewhere, as if a clever maneuverer, a cybernetics expert of the tone, still kept the illusion of governing a mechanism and of watching over a gauge for the time of a turn. I could have spoken of a boom for waters that are not very navigable. This boom is always threatening to give way. I was the first to be afraid of my own voice, as if it were not mine, and to contest it, even to detest it.

If I have always trembled before what I could say, it was fundamentally [*au fond*] because of the tone, and not the substance [*non du fond*]. And what, obscurely, I seek to impart as if in spite of myself, to give or lend to others as well as to myself, to myself as well as to the other, is perhaps a tone. Everything is summoned from an intonation.

And even earlier still, in what gives its tone to the tone, a rhythm. I think that all in all, it is upon rhythm that I stake everything.

It therefore begins before beginning. That is the incalculable origin of a rhythm. Everything is at stake, but may the loser win.

For, naturally, this hyperbolic taste for the purity of language is something I also contracted at school. I am not unaware of that, and it is what needed to be demonstrated. The same goes for hyperbole in general. An incorrigible hyperbolite. A generalized hyperbolite. In short, I exaggerate. I always exaggerate. But as with illnesses caught at school, common sense and doctors recall that predispositions are necessary for their contraction. The presence of a fertile ground must be presumed. No revolt against any discipline, no critique of the academic institution could have silenced what in me will always resemble some last will, the last language of the last word of the last will: speak in good French, in pure French, even at the moment of challenging in a million ways everything that is allied to it, and sometimes everything that inhabits it. Without a doubt I contracted this hyperbolism ("more French than the French," more "purely French" than was demanded by the purity of purists even while I am from the very beginning attacking purity and purification in general, and of course the "ultras" of Algeria), this intemperate and compulsive extremism, from school, yes, in the different French schools where I have spent my life. (Look for yourself, is it fortuitous that the institutions that have harbored me, even in so-called Higher Education, have been called "schools" more often than "universities"?)

But as I have just suggested, this excessiveness was probably more archaic in me than the school. Everything must have begun before preschool; it should remain then for me to analyze it closer to my own distant past, but I still feel incapable of this. Nevertheless, I need to think back to that preschool past in order to account for the generality of the "hyperbolism" which will have invaded my life and work. Everything that proceeds under the name of "deconstruction" arises from it, of course; a telegram would suffice for that here, beginning with the "hyperbole" (it's Plato's word) that will have ordered everything, including the reinterpretation of *khōra*, namely, the passage to the very beyond of the passage of the Good or the One beyond being (*hyperbolē . . . epekeina tes ousias*), excess beyond excess: impregnable. Especially, the same hyperbole will have rushed a French Jewish child from Algeria into feeling, and sometimes calling himself, down to the root of the root, before the root, and in ultra-radicality, more *and* less French but also more *and* less Jewish than all the French, all the Jews, and all the Jews of France. And here as well, [more Francophone Maghrebian] than all the Francophone Maghrebians.

Believe me, although I measure the absurdity and presumptuousness of these infantile allegations (such as the "I am the last Jew" in *Circonfession*), I risk them in order to be honest with my interlocutors and myself, with this someone in me who feels things in that way. In that way and no other. Since I always tell the truth, you can believe me.

Naturally, all of this was a movement in movement. The process never stopped accelerating. Things changed at a quicker pace than that of the rhythm of generations. This precipitation lasted a century for the whole of Algeria, less than a century for the Jews of Algeria. A careful diachronic modulation would be therefore necessary for this tale. But there was a strange moment in the course of the same story. For all phenomena of this kind, war precipitates general precipitation. As it did for the periods of offered or withdrawn citizenship, and for the progress of science and technology [*technique*], of surgery, and medicine in general, war remains a formidable "accelerator." In the middle of the war, just after the landing of the Allied forces in North Africa in November 1942, we witnessed the constitution of a sort of literary capital of France in exile at Algiers: a cultural effervescence, the presence of "famous" writers, the proliferation of journals and editorial initiatives. This also bestows a more theatrical visibility upon Algerian literature of—as they call it—French expression, whether one is dealing with writers of European origin (such as Camus and many others) or with writers of Algerian origin, who constitute a very different mutation. Several years later, in the still-sparkling wake of this strange moment of glory, I seemed to be harpooned by French philosophy and literature, the one and the other, the one or the other: wooden or metallic darts [*flèches*], a penetrating body of enviable, formidable, and inaccessible words even when they were entering me, sentences which it was necessary to appropriate, domesticate, coax [*amadouer*], that is to say, love by setting on fire, burn ("tinder" [*amadou*] is never far away), perhaps destroy, in all events mark, transform, prune, cut, forge, graft at the fire, let come in another way, in other words, to itself in itself.

Let us be more precise. Without a doubt, the coaxing [*amadouer*] was, in this case, a dream. It still remains a dream. What dream? Not that of harming the language (there is nothing I respect and love as much), not that of endangering or injuring it in one of these impulses of revenge out of which I here shape [*fais*] my theme (without ever managing to determine the place of the resentment; who is avenging themselves on whom, and is language itself not borne [*portée*] by this vindictive jealousy?), not that of maltreating this language, in its grammar, its syntax, its lexicon, in the body of rules and norms which constitute its law, nor in the erection that was constituting it into a law by itself. But the dream, which must have started to be dreamt, at that time, was perhaps to make something happen to this language. The desire to make it arrive here, by making something happen to it, to this language that has remained intact, always venerable and venerated, worshipped in the prayer of its words and in the obligations that are contracted in it, by making something happen to it, therefore, something so intimate that it would no longer even be in the position to protest without having to protest, by the same token, against its own emanation, so intimate that it cannot oppose it otherwise than through hideous and shameful symptoms, something so intimate that it comes to take pleasure in it as in itself, at the time it loses itself by finding itself, by converting itself to itself, as the One who turns on itself, who returns (from itself) to itself, at the time when an incomprehensible guest, a newcomer without assignable origin, would make the said language come to him, forcing the language then to speak itself by itself, in another way, in his language. To speak by itself. But for him, and on his terms, keeping in her body the ineffaceable archive of this event: not necessarily an infant but a tattoo, a splendid form, concealed under garments in which blood mixes with ink to reveal all its colors to the sight.[8] The incarnate archive of a liturgy whose secret no one will betray. One that no other person could really appropriate. Not even I, who would, however, be in on the secret.

I must still dream about it, in my "nostalgeria."

I had had to call that my independence from Algeria.

But as I have already said, that was only a first circle of generality, a program common to all the pupils from the moment they *found themselves* subjugated and developed by this pedagogy of French. In a word, from the moment they found themselves.

Within this group, itself deprived of easily accessible models of identification, it is possible to distinguish one of the subgroups to which I belonged to a certain degree. Only to a certain degree, for as soon as one is dealing with questions of culture, language, or writing, the concept of group or class can no longer give rise to a simple topic of exclusion, inclusion, or belonging. This quasi-subgroup will then be that of "indigenous Jews," as they were then called. Being French citizens from 1870 until the laws of exclusion of 1940, they could not properly *identify themselves*, in the double sense of "identifying oneself" and "identifying oneself with" the other. They could not identify themselves in the terms of models, norms, or values whose development was to them alien because French, metropolitan, Christian, and Catholic. In the milieu where I lived, we used to say "the Catholics"; we called all the non-Jewish French people "Catholics," even if they were sometimes Protestants, or perhaps even Orthodox: "Catholic" meant anyone who was neither a Jew, a Berber, nor an Arab. At that time, these young indigenous Jews could easily identify neither with the "Catholics," the Arabs, nor the Berbers, whose language they did not generally speak in that generation. Two generations before them, some of their grandparents still spoke Arabic, at least a certain form of Arabic.

But being already strangers to the roots of French culture, even if that was their only acquired culture, their only educational instruction, and, especially, their only language, being strangers, still more radically, for the most part, to Arab or Berber cultures, the greater majority of these young "indigenous Jews" remained, in addition, strangers to Jewish culture: a strangely bottomless alienation of the soul: a catastrophe; others will also say a paradoxical opportunity. Such, in any event, would have been the radical lack of culture [*inculture*] from which I undoubtedly never completely emerged. From which I emerge without emerging from it, by emerging from it completely without my having ever emerged from it.

There, too, a kind of interdict will have imposed its unwritten law. Since the end of the last century, with the granting of French citizenship, assimilation, as we say, and acculturation—the feverish bid for a "Frenchifying" which was also an embourgeoisification—were so frantic and so careless that the inspiration of Jewish culture seemed to succumb to an *asphyxia*: a state of apparent death, a ceasing of respiration, a fainting fit, a cessation of the pulse. But that was only one of two alternating symptoms of the same affection, for the next moment the pulse seemed to quicken, as if the same "community" had been drugged, intoxicated, inebriated by the new richness. Its memory had, by the same token, been voided, transferred, or transvoided: a million signs prove that. It was struggling to give up the ghost, but in order to incorporate another one as quickly as possible. Unless this movement had been started earlier, exposing this Jewish community in advance to colonial expropriation. I am not in a position, fairly and spontaneously, to put this last hypothesis to the test: because I carry the negative heritage, if I may say so, of this amnesia, which I never had the courage, the strength, and the means to resist, and because an original historian's work would be necessary, of which I have felt myself incapable. Maybe for that very reason.

This incapacity, this handicapped memory, is the subject of my lament here. That is my grievance. For as I thought I perceived it during my adolescent years, when I was beginning to understand a little what was happening, this heritage was already ossified, even necrotized, into ritual comportment, whose meaning was no longer legible even to the majority of the Jews of Algeria. I used to think then that I was dealing with a Judaism of "external signs." But I could not rebel—and believe me, I was rebelling against what I took to be gesticulations, particularly on feast days in the synagogues—I could not lose my temper, except from what was already an insidious Christian contamination: the respectful belief in inwardness, the preference for intention, the heart, the mind, mistrust with respect to literalness or to an objective action given to the mechanicity of the body, in short, a denunciation, so conventional, of Pharisaism.

I will not dwell on these matters, which are all too well known and from which I am very much recovered. But I am evoking them in passing only to point out that I was not the only one to be affected by this Christian "contamination." Social and religious behavior, even Jewish rituals themselves were tainted by them, in their tangible objectivity. The churches were being mimicked, the rabbi would wear a black cassock, and the verger [*chemasch*] a Napoleonic cocked hat; the "bar mitzvah" was called "communion," and circumcision was named "baptism." Things have changed a little since then, but I am referring to the thirties, the forties, and the fifties.

As for language in the strict sense, we could not even resort to some familiar substitute, to some idiom internal to the Jewish community, to any sort of language of refuge that, like Yiddish, would have ensured an element of intimacy, the protection of a "home-of-one's-own" [*un "chez-soi"*] against the language of official culture, a second auxiliary in different socio-semiotic situations. "Ladino" was not spoken in the Algeria I knew, especially not in the big cities like Algiers, where the Jewish population happened to be concentrated.[9]

In a word, here was a disintegrated "community," cut up and cut off. One can imagine the desire to efface such an event or, at the very least, to attenuate it, to make up for it, and also to disclaim it. But whether the desire is fulfilled or not, the traumatism will have taken place, with its indefinite consequences, at once destructuring and structuring. This "community" will have been three times dissociated by what, a little hastily, we are calling interdicts. (1) First of all, it was cut off from both Arabic or Berber (more properly Maghrebian) language and culture. (2) It was also cut off from French, and even European language and culture, which, from its viewpoint, only constituted a distanced pole or metropole, heterogeneous to its history. (3) It was cut off, finally, or to begin with, from Jewish memory, and from the history and language that one must presume to be their own, but which, at a certain point, no longer was. At least not in a typical way for the majority of its members, and not in a sufficiently "lively" and internal way.

A triple dissociation for what one must, however, continue, through a fiction whose simulacrum and cruelty constitute our subject here, to designate the same "community," in the same "country," the same "Republic," three departments of the same "nation-state."

Where then *are we*? Where do we find ourselves? With whom can we still *identify* in order to affirm our own identity and to tell ourselves our own history? First of all, to whom do we recount it? One would have to construct oneself, one would have to be able to *invent oneself* without a model and without an assured addressee. This addressee can, of course, only ever be presumed, in all situations of the world. But the schemas of this presumption were in this case so rare, so obscure, and so random that the word "invention" seems hardly exaggerated.

If I have described these premises well, then what is monolingualism, my "*own*" monolingualism?

My attachment to the French language takes forms that I sometimes consider "neurotic." I feel lost outside the French language. The other languages which, more or less clumsily, I read, decode, or sometimes speak, are languages I shall never inhabit. Where "inhabiting" begins to mean something to me. And dwelling [*demeurer*]. Not only am I lost, fallen, and condemned outside the French language, I have the feeling of honoring or serving all idioms, in a word, of writing the "most" and the "best" when I sharpen the resistance of *my* French, the secret "purity" of my French, the one I was speaking about earlier on, hence its resistance, its *relentless* resistance to translation; translation into *all* languages, including another such French.

Not that I am cultivating the untranslatable. Nothing is untranslatable, however little time is given to the expenditure or expansion of a competent discourse that measures itself against the power of the original. But the "untranslatable" remains—should remain, as my law tells me—the poetic economy of the idiom, the one that is important to me, for I would die even more quickly without it, and which is important to me, myself to myself, where a given formal "quantity" always fails to restore the singular event of the original, that is, to let it be forgotten once recorded, to carry away its number, the prosodic shadow of its quantum. Word for word, if you like, syllable by syllable. From the moment this economic equivalence—strictly impossible, by the way—is renounced, everything can be translated, but in a loose translation, in the loose sense of the word "translation." I am not even talking about poetry, only about prosody, about metrics (accent and quantity in the time of pronunciation). In a sense, nothing is untranslatable; but *in another sense*, everything is untranslatable; translation is another name for the impossible. In another sense of the word "translation," of course, and from one sense to the other—it is easy for me always to hold firm between these two hyperboles which are fundamentally the same, and always translate each other.

How can one say and how can one know, with a certainty that is at one with oneself, that one shall never inhabit the language of the other, the other language, when it is the only language that one speaks, and speaks in monolingual obstinacy, in a jealously and severely idiomatic way, without, however, being ever at home in it? And that the jealous guard that one mounts in proximity to one's language, even as one is denouncing the nationalist politics of language (I do the one and the other), demands the multiplication of shibboleths as so many challenges to translations, so many taxes levied on the frontier of languages, so many alliances assigned to the ambassadors of the idiom, so many inventions ordered for translators: therefore invent in *your* language if you can or want to hear mine; invent if you can or want to give my language to be understood, as well as yours, where the event of its prosody only takes place once at home, in the very place where its "being home" [*son "chez elle"*] disturbs the co-inhabitants, the fellow citizens, and the compatriots? Compatriots of every country, translator-poets, rebel against patriotism! Do you hear me! Each time I write a word, a word that I love and love to write; in the time of this word, at the instant of a single syllable, the song of this new International awakens in me. I never resist it, I am in the street at its call, even if, apparently, I have been working silently since dawn at my table.

But above all, and here is the most fatal question: How is it possible that this language, the only language that this monolingual speaks, and is destined to speak, forever and ever, is not his? How can one believe that it remains always mute for the one who inhabits it, and whom it inhabits most intimately, that it remains *distant, heterogeneous, uninhabitable, deserted*? Deserted like a desert in which one must grow, make things grow, build, and project up to the idea of a route, and the trace of a return, *yet another language*?

I say route and trace of a return, for what distinguishes a route from a path or from a *via rupta* (its *etymon*), as well as *methodos* from *odos*, is repetition, return, reversibility, iter-ability, the possible reiteration of the itinerary. How is it possible that, whether received or learned, this language is felt, explored, worked, and to be reinvented without an itinerary, and without a map, like the language of the other?

I do not know whether there is arrogance or modesty in claiming that such was, in a large measure, my experience, or that it resembles my destiny a little, at least with regard to its difficulty.

But I will be told, not without reason, that it is *always that way a priori*—and for everyone else. The language called maternal is never purely natural, nor proper, nor inhabitable. *To inhabit*: this is a value that is quite *disconcerting* and equivocal; one never inhabits what one is in the habit of calling inhabiting. There is no possible habitat without the difference of this exile and this nostalgia. Most certainly. That is all too well known. But it does not follow that all exiles are equivalent. From this shore, yes, *from this* shore or this common drift, all expatriations remain singular.

For there is a twist to this truth. This a priori universal truth of an essential alienation in language—which is always of the other—and, by the same token, in all culture. This necessity is here re-marked, therefore marked, and revealed one more time, still one more first time, in an incomparable setting. A setting called historical and singular, one which appears idiomatic, which determines and phenomenalizes it by bringing it back to itself.

All these words: *truth, alienation, appropriation, habitation, one's-home* [*chez-soi*], *ipseity, place of the subject, law,* and so on remain, in my eyes, problematic. Without exception. They bear the stamp of the metaphysics that imposed itself through, precisely, *this* language of the other, *this* monolingualism of the other. So much so that this debate with monolingualism will have been nothing other than a piece of *deconstructive* writing [*écriture*]. Such writing always attacks the body of this language, my only language, and what it bears the most or in the best way, namely, the philosophical tradition that supplies us with the reservoir of concepts I definitely have to use, and that I have indeed had to serve for a short while now in order to describe this situation, even in the distinction between transcendental or ontological universality and phenomenal empiricity.

Why emphasize this last distinction? Because among so many paradoxical effects, there would be the following, of which I am indicating only the principle. I would now like to show that this empirico-transcendental or ontico-ontological re-mark, this folding which imprints itself upon the enigmatic articulation between a universal structure and its idiomatic testimony, reverses all the signs without any hesitation.

The break with tradition, uprooting, the inaccessibility of histories, amnesia, indecipherability, and so on: all of these unleash the genealogical drive, the desire of the idiom, the compulsive impulse to anamnesis, and the destructive love of the interdict. What I was calling just a while ago the tattooing of all colors on the body when they are allowed to be seen. The absence of a stable model of identification for an *ego*—in all its dimensions: linguistic, cultural, and so on—gives rise to impulses that are always *on the brink* of collapse and oscillate, as a result, between three threatening possibilities:

1. an amnesia without recourse, under the guise of pathological destructuring, growing disintegration: a madness;

2. stereotypes that homogenize and conform to the model of the "average" or dominant French person, another amnesia under the integrative guise, another type of madness;

3. the madness of a hypermnesia, a supplement of loyalty, a surfeit, or even excrescence of memory, to commit oneself, at the limit of the two other possibilities, to traces—traces of writing, language, experience—which carry anamnesis beyond the mere reconstruction of a given heritage, beyond an available past. Beyond any cartography, and beyond any knowledge that can be taught. At stake there is an entirely other anamnesis, and, if one may say so, even an anamnesis of the entirely other, about which I would like to explain myself a little.

This is the most difficult thing. It should permit me to return to my initial and apparently contradictory propositions, but it involves another thought of avowal or confession, of the "truthmaking" that I might have outlined in *Circonfession*, next to a mother who was dying while losing her memory, her speech, and her power of naming.

Let us sum up. The monolingual of whom I speak speaks a language of which he is *deprived*. The French language is not his. Because he is therefore deprived of *all* language, and no longer has any other recourse—neither Arabic, nor Berber, nor Hebrew, nor any languages his ancestors would have spoken—because this monolingual is in a way *aphasic* (perhaps he writes because he is an aphasic), he is thrown into absolute translation, a translation without a pole of reference, without an originary language, and without a source language [*langue de départ*]. For him, there are only target languages [*langues d'arrivée*], if you will, the remarkable experience being, however, that these languages just cannot manage to reach themselves because they no longer know where they are coming from, what they are speaking *from* and what the sense of their journey is. Languages without an itinerary and, above all, without any superhighway of goodness knows what information.

As if there were only arrivals [*arrivées*], and therefore only events without arrival. From these sole "arrivals," and from these arrivals alone, desire springs forth; since desire is borne by the arrival itself, it springs forth even before the ipseity of an *I-me* that would bear it in advance; it springs forth, and even sets itself up as a desire to reconstruct, to restore, but it is really a desire to invent a *first language* that would be, rather, a *prior-to-the-first* language destined to translate that memory. But to translate the memory of what, precisely, did not take place, of what, having been (the) forbidden, ought, nevertheless, to have left a trace, a specter, the phantomatic body, the phantom-member—palpable, painful, but hardly legible—of traces, marks, and scars. As if it were a matter of producing the truth of what never took place by avowing it. What then is this avowal, and the age-old error or originary defect from which one must write?

Invented for the genealogy of what did not happen and whose event will have been absent, leaving only negative traces of itself in what *makes history*, such a *prior-to-the-first* language does not exist. It is not even a preface, a "foreword," or some lost language of origin. It can only be a target or, rather, a future language, a promised sentence, a language of the other, once again, but entirely other than the language of the other as the language of the master or colonist, even though, between them, the two may sometimes show so many unsettling resemblances maintained in secret or held in reserve.

"Unsettling," for this ambiguity will never be removed: in the eschatological or messianic horizon that this promise cannot deny—or that it can merely deny—the prior-to-the-first language can always run the risk of becoming or wanting to be another language of the master, sometimes that of new masters. It is at each instant of writing or reading, at each moment of poetic experience that the decision must arise against a background of the undecidable. It is often a political decision—and often a decision regarding the political side of things. As a condition of the decision as well as that of responsibility, the undecidable inscribes threat in chance, and terror in the ipseity of the host.

Perhaps this is the place for *two remarks*, one of them being more typological or taxonomical, and the other more legibly political, without the shadow of a doubt.

1. Let us emphasize once more what distinguishes this situation from that of Franco-Maghrebians or, more precisely, from that of Francophone Maghrebian writers who have access to their presumed mother tongue. This resource has been remarkably described by Khatibi. His analysis appears at once close to and different, in a subtle way, from the one I am attempting here:

> Every language proposes several modes, directions, and sites to (its) thought, and the attempt to keep this entire chain under the law of the One will have been the millennial history of metaphysics, of which Islam represents here the mystical and theological reference par excellence.

Yet, in this story ["Talismano," by Abdelwahab Meddeb], which is transcribed between a diglossia and a dead language, what would it be to think in accordance with this unifying direction (in the French language)? And, from our perspective, what would it be to think in accordance with this riddle [*cet incalculable*]: from three, derive the one, and from the one, the median, the other, the interval of this palimpsest?

I have suggested . . . that the Arab writer of French expression is caught in a chiasmus, a chiasmus between alienation and inalienation (with emphasis on all senses of these two terms): this author does not write his own language; he transcribes his proper name transformed; he can possess nothing (if there is the remotest chance that one appropriates any language at all); he possesses neither his *maternal dialect, which is not written* [my italics; J. D.: if he does not possess his maternal dialect *insofar as it is not written*, at least he "possesses" it as a "spoken" idiom, which is not the case of the Jew of Algeria, whose maternal dialect—being already the language of the other, of the non-Jewish French colonist—literally lacks the unity, the age, and the presumed proximity of a maternal dialect], nor the written Arabic language, which is alienated and given to a substitution, nor this other acquired language [*langue apprise*], in which he is beckoned to dispossess and to efface himself. Irremediable suffering results when this writer does not assume this broached identity, in *a lucidity of thought that lives on this chiasmus, on this schism* [schize]."[10]

2. In spite of appearances, this exceptional situation is, at the same time, certainly exemplary of a universal structure; it represents or reflects a type of originary "alienation" that institutes every language as a language of the other: the impossible property of a language. But that must not lead to a kind of neutralization of differences, to the misrecognition of determinate expropriations against which a war can be waged on quite different fronts. On the contrary, that is what allows the stakes to be repoliticized. Where neither natural property nor the law of property in gen-

eral exist, where this de-propriation is recognized, it is possible and it becomes more necessary than ever occasionally to identify, in order to combat them, impulses, phantasms, "ideologies," "fetishizations," and symbolics of appropriation. Such a reminder permits one at once to analyze the historical phenomena of appropriation and to treat them *politically* by avoiding, above all, the reconstitution of what these phantasms managed to motivate: "nationalist" aggressions (which are always more or less "naturalist") or monoculturalist homo-hegemony.

Since the prior-to-the-first time of pre-originary language does not exist, it must be invented. Injunctions, the summons [*mise en demeure*] of another writing. But, above all, it must be written *within* languages, so to speak. One must summon up writing inside the given language. From the cradle to the grave, that language, for me, will have been French.

By definition, I no longer know how, and have never been able, to say that it is a good or a bad thing. It just happened that way. Lastingly [*à demeure*].

The obscure chance, my good fortune, a gift for which thanks should be given to goodness knows what archaic power, is that it was always easier for me to bless this destiny. Much easier, more often than not, and even now, to bless than to curse it. The day I would get to know to whom gratitude must be rendered for it, I would know everything, and I would be able to die in peace. Everything I do, especially when I am writing, resembles a game of blindman's buff: the one who is writing, always by hand, even when using machines, holds out his hand like a blind man seeking to touch the one whom he could thank for the gift of a language, for the very words in which he declares himself ready to give thanks. And to beg for mercy as well.

While the other, more prudent, hand, another blindman's hand, tries to protect against the fall, against a headlong, premature fall, in a word, against haste. I have been saying for a long time now that one writes manuscripts for two hands. And I digitize like a madman.

But this disconcerting intimacy, this place "inside" the French language could *not* not, lo and behold, inscribe in the relationship to itself of the language, in its auto-affection, so to speak, an absolute outside, a *zone* outside the law, the cleaved enclave of a barely audible or legible reference to that *entirely other* prior-to-the-first language, to that degree *zero-minus-one* of writing [*écriture*] that leaves its phantomatical map "inside" the said monolanguage. That too is a peculiar phenomenon of translation. The translation of a language that does not as yet exist, and that will never have existed, in any given target language [*dans une langue à l'arrivée donnée*].

This translation translates itself in an internal (Franco-French) translation by playing with the non-identity with itself of all language. By playing and taking pleasure [*en jouissant*].

No such thing as *a* language exists. At present. Nor does the language. Nor the idiom or dialect. That, moreover, is why one would never be able *to count* these things, and why if, in a sense I shall explain in a moment, we only ever have one language, this monolingualism is not at one with itself.

For the classical linguist, of course, each language is a system whose unity is always reconstituted. But this unity is not comparable to any other. It is open to the most radical grafting, open to deformations, transformations, expropriation, to a certain a-nomie and de-regulation. So much so that the gesture—here, once again, I am calling it writing [*écriture*], even though it can remain purely oral, vocal, and musical: rhythmic or prosodic—that seeks to affect monolanguage, the one that one has without having it, is always multiple. It dreams of leaving there marks that recall that entirely other language, in short, that degree zero-minus-one of memory.

This gesture is in itself plural, divided, and overdetermined. It can always allow itself to be interpreted as an impulse of love or aggression toward the body of any given language that is thus exposed. Actually, it does both things; it surrenders itself, devotes itself, and links itself together with the given language, in this case, French, and in French, in order to give it what the language does not have and what the gesture itself does not have. But this *salvation*—for it is a salvation addressed to the mortality of the other and a desire for infinite salvation—is also a scratch and a grafting. It caresses with claws, sometimes borrowed claws.

If, for example, I dream of writing an anamnesis of what enabled me to identify myself or say *I* from depths of amnesia and aphasia, I know, by the same token, that I can do it only by opening up an impossible path, leaving the road, escaping, giving myself the slip, inventing a language different enough to disallow its own *reappropriation* within the norms, the body, and the law of the given language—or by all the normative schemas constituted by programs of a grammar, a lexicon, a semantics, a rhetoric, speech genres or literary forms, stereotypes or cultural clichés (the most authoritarian of which remain mechanisms of avant-gardist reproducibility, and the indefatigable regeneration of the literary superego). The improvisation of some inaugurality is, without the shadow of a doubt, the impossible itself. Reappropriation always takes place. As it remains inevitable, the aporia involves a language that is impossible, unreadable, and inadmissible. An untranslatable translation. At the same time, this untranslatable translation, this new idiom *makes things happen* [*fait arriver*], this signature brought forth [*fait arrivée*], produces events in the given language, the given language to which things must still be given, sometimes *unverifiable* events: illegible events. Events that are always promised rather than given. Messianic events. But the promise is not nothing; it is not a non-event.

How does one account for this logic? How does one keep this account or this *logos*? Although I have often made use of the expression "the given language" in order to speak of an available monolanguage—for example, French—there is no given language, or rather there is some language, a gift of language (*es gibt die Sprache*), but there is not a language. Not a given one. It does not exist. Like the hospitality of the host even before any invitation, it summons when summoned. Like a charge [*enjoignante*], it remains to be given, it remains only on this condition: by still remaining to be given.

Let us turn then, one more time, to that somewhat sententious proposition: "We only ever have one language." Let us take it through one more round. Let it us make it say what it does not know how to mean to say, and let us allow it to say something else.

One can, of course, speak several languages. There are speakers who are competent in more than one language. Some even write several languages at a time (prostheses, grafts, translation, transposition). But do they not always do it with a view to an absolute idiom? and in the promise of a still unheard-of language? of a sole poem previously inaudible?

Each time I open my mouth, each time I speak or write, I *promise*. Whether I like it or not: here, the fatal precipitation of the promise must be dissociated from the values of the will, intention, or meaning-to-say that are reasonably attached to it. The performative of this promise is not one speech act among others. It is implied by any other performative, and this promise heralds the uniqueness of a language to come. It is the "there must be a language" (which necessarily implies: "for it does not exist," or "since it is lacking"), "I promise a language," "a language is promised," which at once precedes all language, summons all speech and already belongs to each language as it does to all speech.

This appeal to come [*appel à venir*] gathers language together in advance. It welcomes it, collects it, not in its identity or its unity, not even in its ipseity, but in the uniqueness or singularity of a gathering together of its difference to itself: in difference *with itself* [*avec soi*] rather than difference *from itself* [*d'avec soi*]. It is not possible to speak outside this promise[11] that gives *a* language, the uniqueness of the idiom, but only by promising to give it. There can be no question of getting out of this *uniqueness without unity*. It is not to be opposed to the other, nor even distinguished from the other. It is the monolanguage *of* the other. The *of* signifies not so much property as provenance: language is for the other, coming from the other, *the* coming of the other.

The promise of which I speak, the one of which I was saying above that it remains threatening (contrary to what is generally thought about the promise) and of which I am now proposing that it promises the impossible but also the possibility of all speech; this strange promise neither yields nor delivers any messianic or eschatological *content* here. There is no salvation here that saves or promises salvation, even if on the hither or the other side of any soteriology, this promise resembles the salvation addressed to the other, the other recognized as an entirely different other (the entirely other is entirely other where a knowledge or recognition does not suffice for it), the other recognized as mortal, finite, in a state of neglect, and deprived of any horizon of hope.

But the fact that there is no necessarily determinable *content* in this promise of the other, and in the language of the other, does not make any less indisputable its opening up of speech by something that *resembles* messianism, soteriology, or eschatology. It is the structural opening, the messiani*city*, without which *messianism* itself, in the strict or literal sense, would not be possible. Unless, perhaps, this originary promise without any proper content is, precisely, messianism. And unless all messianism demands for itself this rigorous and barren severity, this messianicity shorn of everything. Let us never rule it out.

There, too, we would be faced with a *remark* of the universal structure: the messianic idiom of some religion or other would re-discover its imprint there. We would be faced with the becoming-exemplary that each religion bears in its heart, on the very grounds of this remarkability. This monolingualism of the other certainly has the threatening face and features of colonial hegemony. But what remains insurmountable in it, whatever the necessity or legitimacy of all the emancipations, is quite simply the "there is language," a "there is language which does not exist," namely that there is no metalanguage, and that *a* language shall always be called upon to speak about *the* language—*because* the latter does not exist. It does not henceforth exist; it never exists yet. What a time [*temps*, meaning tense and also weather]! What sort of weather it is; what the weather is like in this language that fails, lastingly [*à demeure*], to reach home.

You can translate such a necessity in several ways, into more than one language, for example, in the idiom of Novalis or Hei-degger when they speak [*disent*], each in his own way, the *Mono-logue* of a speech that always speaks of itself. As recalled elsewhere, Heidegger explicitly declared the absence of all metalanguage. This is not to say that language is monological and tautological, but that it is always up to a language to summon the heterologi-cal opening that permits it to speak of something else and to address itself to the other. It can also be translated into the idiom of Celan, the poet-translator who, while writing in the language of the other, and about the Holocaust, while inscribing Babel in the very body of each poem, expressly claimed, signed, and sealed the poetic monolingualism of his work just the same. It can also be given over, without betrayal, to other inventions of idioms, to other poetics, without end.

Epilogue

One more word to expatiate a bit. What I am sketching here is, above all, not the beginning of some autobiographical or anamnestic outline, nor even a timid essay toward an intellectual bildungsroman. Rather than an exposition of myself, it is an account of what will have placed an obstacle in the way of this auto-exposition for me. An account, therefore, of what will have exposed me to that obstacle and thrown me against it. Of a serious traffic accident about which I never cease thinking.

Certainly, everything that has, say, interested me for a long time—on account of writing, the trace, the deconstruction of phallogocentrism and "the" Western metaphysics (which I have never identified, regardless of whatever has been repeated about it ad nauseum, as a single homogeneous thing watched over by its definite article in the singular; I have so often and so explicitly said the opposite!)—all of that could *not* not proceed from the strange reference to an "elsewhere" of which the place and the language were unknown and prohibited even to myself, as if I were trying to *translate* into the only language and the only French Western culture that I have at my disposal, the culture into which I was thrown at birth, a possibility that is inaccessible to myself, as if I were trying to translate a speech I did not yet know into my "monolanguage," as if I were still weaving some veil from the wrong side (which many weavers do, I might add), and as if the necessary passage points of this weaving from the wrong side were places of *transcendence*, of an absolute elsewhere, therefore, in the eyes of Graeco-Latino-Christian Western philosophy, but yet *inside it* (*epekeina tes ousias*, and beyond—*khōra*—negative theology, Meister Eckhart and beyond, Freud and beyond, a certain Heidegger, Artaud, Levinas, Blanchot, and certain others).

Certainly. But I would not be able to account for it from the individual situation I have just described so schematically. That cannot be explained from the individual journey, that of the young Franco-Maghrebian Jew of a certain generation. The paths and strategies that I have had to follow in this work or passion also follow the dictates of some structures and therefore of some assignations that are internal to the Graeco-Latino-Christiano-Gallic culture to which my monolingualism forever confines me; it was necessary to reckon with this culture in order to translate, attract, and seduce into it the very thing, the "elsewhere," toward which I was myself ex-ported in advance, namely the "elsewhere" of this altogether other with which I have had to keep, in order to keep myself but also in order to keep myself from it, as from a fearsome promise, a sort of relationship without a relationship, with one guarding itself from the other, in the waiting without horizon for a language that only knows how to keep people waiting.

That is all it knows how to do, to keep people waiting, and that is all I know about it. Even today and, without the shadow of a doubt, for good.

All *the* languages of "the" aforementioned Western metaphysics, for there is more than one, and even the proliferating lexicons of deconstruction and so on and so forth belong, by virtue of almost all the tattooing on their bodies, to that deal [*donne*] with which one must thus explain oneself.

A Judeo-Franco-Maghrebian genealogy does not clarify everything, far from it. But could I explain anything without it, ever? No, nothing, nothing of what preoccupies me, what engages me, what keeps me in motion or in "communication," nothing of what summons me sometimes across the silent time of interrupted communications, nothing, moreover, of what isolates me in a kind of almost involuntary retreat, a desert that I sometimes have the illusion of "cultivating" by myself, of surveying *like* a desert, while furnishing myself with fine and nice excuses — what little taste, but also what "ethics," what "politics"! — whereas a hostage's place was reserved there for me, as a summons [*mise en demeure*], right before me.

The miracle of translation does not take place every day; there is, at times, a desert without a desert crossing. And that, perhaps, is what today, in the confines of Parisian culture, certainly, but already in Western "mediatization," indeed, on the very highways of the ongoing globalization of "public space," one so often calls unreadability.

What, then, are the chances of the readability of such a discourse against its unreadability? For I do not know whether what you have just heard me say will be intelligible. Either where, when, or to whom. Or to what extent. Perhaps I have just made a "demonstration"; it is not certain, but I no longer know in what language to understand that word. Without an accent, a demonstration is not a logical argumentation that imposes a conclusion; it is, first of all, a political event, a demonstration in the street (a short while ago, I mentioned how I take to the streets every morning; never to the highway, but to the streets), a march, an act, an appeal, a demand. That is, one more scene. I have just made a scene. In French, too, the *démonstration*, with an accent, can be, first and foremost, a gesture, a movement of the body, the act of a "manifestation." Yes, a scene. A street scene without a theater, yet a scene all the same. What I am entertaining doubts about, supposing it is of interest to anyone at all, would be the extent to which that scene betrays me, the extent to which, from one listening about which I have no idea, you will hear from it what I meant neither to say, nor to teach, nor to make known, in good French.

—Are you then promising me a discourse on the still-readable secrets of unreadability? Will there be someone to hear it again?

—Quite a long time ago, that, put in different words, would have resembled for me a terrifying children's game, unforgettable overthere, interminable. I have left it behind overthere; I shall tell you about it one day. Its living voice has grown husky, a very young voice, but it is not dead. It is not an evil. I have the feeling that, if it is given back to me one day, I shall then see, for the first time in reality, as a prisoner of the cave does after death, the truth of what I have lived: *the truth itself* beyond memory, as the hidden other side of shadows, of images, of images of images, and of phantasms that have filled each moment of my life.

I am not talking about the brevity of a recorded film that one could see again (life will have been so short) but of the very thing itself.

Beyond memory and time lost. I am not even speaking of an ultimate unveiling, but of what will have remained alien, for all time, to the veiled figure, to the very figure of the veil.

This desire and promise let all my specters loose. A desire without a horizon, for that is its luck or its condition. And a promise that no longer expects what it waits for: there where, striving for what is given to come, I finally know how not to have to distinguish any longer between promise and terror.

Notes

Notes

1. Abdelkebir Khatibi, *Du bilinguisme* (Paris: Denoël, 1985), p. 10.

2. Benveniste reconstitutes and displays this chain in several places, notably in a magnificent chapter entitled "L'hospitalité," in *Le vocabulaire des institutions indo-européennes* (Paris: Minuit, 1969), vol. 1, pp. 87ff., a chapter to which I shall perhaps return elsewhere in a more problematic and troubled way.

3. What is thus formulated about the promise as threat risked and no doubt still risks appearing rather dogmatic and obscure. On this point, I refer the reader to a more sustained and hopefully more convincing argumentation in "Avances," preface to Serge Margel, *Le tombeau du dieu artisan* (Paris: Minuit, 1995).

4. To shed a little light on this insistent use of the idiom linked to dwelling [*demeure*], I refer the reader to "Demeure" in *Passions de la littérature* (Paris: Galilée, 1996), pp. 13–74.

5. On dissemination as an experience of uniqueness and dissemination in accordance with folds, or with fold upon fold, see *La dissémination* (Paris: Seuil, 1972), pp. 50, 259, 283, 291ff. and passim.

6. Abdelkebir Khatibi, *Amour bilingue* (Montpellier: Fata Morgana, 1983), p. 75; translated as *Love in Two Languages* by Richard Howard (Minneapolis: University of Minnesota Press, 1990). All translations from this text are, however, mine — Trans.

7. On this juridical notion as well as the extraordinary history of citizenship in Algeria (which has, to my knowledge, no other equivalent *strictu sensu*, in the world) I refer to the luminous article by Louis-Augustin Barrière, "Le puzzle de la citoyenneté en Algérie," published

in the journal of Gisti (*Plein droit*, nos. 29–30, November 1995), whose work, today recognized as exemplary, I would like to commend in passing. This article (which must be read in its entirety) begins as follows: "Until the Liberation, Muslims of Algeria were considered only to be French Nationals and not to be French citizens. That distinction was explained through history."

8. At the time of re-reading page proofs, I see on television a Japanese film whose name I do not know, which tells the story of a tattoo artist. His masterpiece: an extraordinary tattoo with which he is covering the back of his wife while making love to her, from behind, having understood that such was the condition of his "*ductus.*" He is seen pushing in his pin while his wife, who is lying flat on her belly, turns a suppliant and pained face toward him. She leaves him because of this violence. But later she sends him the son she took away from him, although at first he does not recognize this son, so that he can make a master tattooist of him, too. Henceforth, the artist-father cannot work on the back of another woman except by making her lie on his son, a son as handsome as a god, a son whom he still has not recognized but whom he calls by his name at each moment of great pain. This call is a command, a command for him to provide more compensatory pleasure to the young woman, the prop or subject of the operation, a suffering subjectile, the passion of the masterpiece. The ending is terrible; I shall not recount it, but only the woman survives, and hence the masterpiece. And the memory of all the promises. She cannot see this masterpiece she is wearing, not directly, and not without a mirror, but it subsists directly on her, at least for some time—lodged [*à demeure*] for a limited time, of course.

9. Supposing that these modest reflections propose to add an example quite common, all in all, to the file of a general study to come, and supposing this study to be of a historical or socioanthropological kind, then in these hypotheses, which will here remain so many hypotheses, one could witness the emergence of a taxonomy or a general typology. Its most ambitious title could be *The Monolingualism of the Host: Jews of the Twentieth Century, the Mother Tongue, and the Language of the Other, on Both Sides of the Mediterranean.* From the coast of this

long note, it is as if I were taking in the view of the other shore of Judaism, on *another* other coastline of the Mediterranean, in places that, in another way, are even more alien to me than Christian France.

The best-known and the most justly famous figures among them are European by birth. And all of them "Ashkenazim," which already poses a number of problems. What will the Sephardic version of this typology be? Furthermore, the diversity of these Ashkenazic Jewish figures of Europe calls for an entangled taxonomy (which I am attempting to study in a seminar on hospitality, and to which I hope to devote a study some day). Before saying a word, however insufficient and out of proportion it might be, of course, about a select few among adventures that were immense and unique (from Kafka to Levinas, from Scholem to Adorno, from Benjamin to Celan and Arendt), let us, in the first place, recall the situation of Franz Rosenzweig. *In the first place* because Rosenzweig proposed a *general* study that puts our problem in perspective; he laid out the question of Jews and "their" foreign language, if I may say so. He did it in a more "theoretical" and formalized manner. Whether one subscribes to his interpretations or not, they offer a precious and systematic topography.

1. **Rosenzweig,** then. Already the "eternal people," unlike all the others, "do not begin with autochthony." The "father from whom Israel descended was an immigrant" (*L'étoile de la rédemption*, trans. A. Derczanski and J.-L. Schlegel [Paris: Seuil, 1982], p. 354). Already they are deprived of a "home of their own" to "sleep" in [*un "chez soi" ou "s'endormir"*], except for the holy and sacred land, which, moreover, is by right the property only of God (p. 355). Above all, they have no language that is exclusively their own, only the language of the host: "the eternal people have lost their own language [*seine eigne Sprache verloren hat*]"; "everywhere they speak the language of their external destinies, for example, the language of the people in whose dwelling place they reside as guests [*bei dem es etwa zu Gaste wohnt*], and when they do not claim the right to hospitality [*das Gastrecht*] and live for themselves in closed colonies [*in geschlossener Siedlung*: we are not dealing here with the colony of 'colonization,' but with 'colony' in the broad

sense of a dwelling place or a conglomeration], they speak the language
of the people from whom they received, when departing, the strength
to undertake this march [*Siedeln*, this establishment]; they never possess this language on the grounds of their belonging to the same blood,
but always as the language of immigrants who have come from everywhere: 'Judeo-Spanish' ['*dzudezmo*'] in the Balkans and '*tatsch*' [another
name for Yiddish] in Eastern Europe are simply the best-known examples today. Consequently, whereas all the other peoples are identified
with their own language, and the language dries up in their mouths on
the day they cease to be a people, Jewish people no longer ever identify
themselves wholly with the language they speak [*wächst das jüdische Volk
mit den Sprachen, die es spricht, nie mehr ganz zusammen*]."

And after a judgment which would merit more than one anxious suspicion, like all his discourse on blood ties, since the one and the other
sometimes closely resemble—though involuntarily, of course, but so
recklessly—anti-Semitic slogans, Rosenzweig concludes that "this language . . . is not theirs [*nicht die eigene ist*: is not their proper language]":
"Even where they speak the language of the host who is accommodating them [*die Sprache des Gatsvolks*], a characteristic vocabulary, or at
least a specific selection from the common vocabulary, peculiar turns of
phrase, a characteristic sense of what is beautiful or ugly in the language
in question, all of this reveals that this language is not theirs" (p. 356).

In the same way as there is a holy land (theirs but not appropriable,
only allotted, lent by God, the only legitimate proprietor of the land),
the holy language, similarly, is theirs only to the extent that they do not
"speak" it, and to the extent that it is employed in prayer (for "they can
only pray" in it) only for *testifying*: "attestation" (*Zeugnis*) that "their
linguistic life always feels (dis)located in an alien land, and that their
personal linguistic fatherland [*seine eigentliche Sprachheimat*] is known
to be elsewhere, in the sphere of the holy language, inaccessible to everyday speech."

(I shall perhaps speak again elsewhere [in *Les yeux de la langue:
L'abîme et le volcan*, forthcoming] about the letter Scholem wrote to
Rosenzweig as a gift on an anniversary day in December 1926 ["Une let-

tre inédite de Gerschom Scholem à Franz Rosenzweig: A propos de notre langue, une confession"], a remarkable text edited and translated by Stephane Moses in *Archives de sciences sociales des religions* 60, no. 1 [July–September 1985]: 83–84. This translation was followed by a precious article by S. Moses, "Langage et sécularisation chez Gerschom Scholem."

This "Confession on the Subject of Our Language" (*Bekenntnis über unsere Sprache*) admits to an anguish in the face of the volcanic eruptions that the modernization, secularization, and, more precisely, "actualization" (*Aktualisierung*) of sacred Hebrew risk producing one day: "This country is a volcano in which language will boil [*Das Land ist ein Vulkan, Es beherbergt die Sprache*]. . . . There exists another danger even more disturbing [*umheimlicher*] than the Arab nation, a danger which is a necessary consequence of the Zionist enterprise: What about the 'actualization' of the Hebrew language; does this sacred language by which our children are nourished not constitute an abyss [*Abgrund*] which will, without fail, open up someday? . . . May we not be running the risk of seeing, someday, the religious power of this language turned violently against those who speak it? . . . As far as we are concerned, we live inside our language, which for most of us is like blind men walking over an abyss. But when vision is granted us, to ourselves and our descendants, shall we not fall to the bottom of this abyss? And no one can tell whether the sacrifice of those who will be destroyed in this fall will be enough to seal it up again."

A spectral voice arises from the bottom of this abyss (*Abgrund*), whose figure, at least five times in the two-page letter, never ceases coming back. The logic of the haunting memory is not fortuitously allied to a linguistics of the name. The essence of speech and, let us add, of language (*Sprache*) is determined by Scholem, as by others— Benjamin or Heidegger for example—*simultaneously* from *sacrality* [*sacralité*] and *nomination*, in two words, from sacred names, from the power of the sacrosanct name: "Language is name [*Sprache ist Namen*]. It is in the name that the power of language is hidden, it is in it that the abyss it contains is sealed [*Im Namen ist die Macht der Sprache beschlossen, ist ihr Abgrund versigelt*]."

After the loss of sacred names, after their apparent disappearance, their spectrality returns; it comes back to haunt our poor speech. "Most certainly, the language we speak is rudimentary, almost ghostly [*wir freilich sprechen eine gespenstische Sprache*]. Names haunt our sentences; writers or journalists play with them, pretending to believe or make believe in God, and that all of this is of no importance [*es habe nichts zu bedeuten*]. And yet in this debased and spectral language, the power of the sacred [*die Kraft des Heiligen*] often seems to speak to us. For names have their own life. If they did not have it, woe betide our children, who would be delivered without hope to an empty future."

Scholem names the danger of this loss more than once: *verdict* and *apocalypse*, the truth, in short, of a last judgment of history.)

How then do we "situate" the discourse of the first addressee of this strange letter? From which place should we hear Rosenzweig, whose *L'étoile de la rédemption* (1921) had already appeared, a text that Scholem, who did not hesitate to fall out with its author, held to be "one of the most important creations of Jewish religious thought of our century" (*De Berlin à Jerusalem*, trans. S. Bollack [Paris: Albin Michel, 1984], pp. 199–200)?

Two minimal remarks on the only features we can retain here: whatever the radicality and generality of this de-propriation of language attributed to the "Jewish people," Rosenzweig *attenuates* it, if one may risk saying this, *in three ways*.

These three ways also indicate three reappropriations prohibited to the "French-Jew-from-Algeria" who speaks, and of whom I am speaking, here.

a. Rosenzweig recalls that the Jewish person can still appropriate and love the language of the host like *their own*, in a country that is their own, and, above all, in a country that is not a "colony," a colony of colonization or military invasion. Rosenzweig noted his *unreserved* attachment to the German language, the language of his country. He did it in all possible ways, to the point of translating the Bible into German. A respectable and terrified rivalry with Luther, "*Gastgeschenk*," acknowledgments, and token of the guest who is giving thanks for received hospitality, as, once again, Scholem said one day: it was at Jerusalem, in Israel, more than thirty years afterwards, in 1961. Scholem was then addressing Buber, Rosenzweig's collaborator in the translation of the Bible, and he was playing on this word *Gastgeschenk*, with as much appropriate admiration as irony and skepticism toward the so-called "Judeo-German" couple. Scholem then adds that this *Gastgeschenk*, namely, a translation, the translation of a sacred text, "will instead be—I am saying this not without displeasure—the tombstone of a relationship that has been annihilated in a horrifying catastrophe. The Jews for whom you have undertaken this translation are no more, and those of their children who escaped that catastrophe no longer read German. . . . The contrast that existed between the language current in 1925 and the one of your translation has not diminished in the course of the last thirty-five years, it has even increased."

A translation of the Bible as a tombstone, a tombstone in the place of a gift from the guest or a gift of hospitality (*Gastgeschenk*), a funerary crypt given in thanks for a language, the tomb of a poem in memory of a language given, a tomb which contains several other ones, including all the ones from the Bible, including the one from the Scriptures (and Rosenzweig was never far from becoming a Christian), the gift of a poem as the offering from a tomb which could be, for all one will ever know, a cenotaph, what an opportunity to commemorate a monolingualism of the other! What a sanctuary, and what a seal, for so many languages!

Scholem politely hints at the suspicion of the cenotaph but it is true that at the end of this extraordinary address it was still necessary for him to quote Hölderlin, too, for him in turn to pay to an unforgettable poem in the German language a homage that I believe is memorable here. The promise or call still allows itself to be understood there: "As for the use to which the Germans will henceforth put your translation, who could predict it? For in the lives of Germans, a lot more has occurred than Hölderlin could have foreseen when he was writing:

> Und nicht übel ist, wenn einiges
> verloren gehet, und von der Rede
> verhullet der lebendige Laut

> It is not an evil thing if something
> endures perdition and the living voice
> of speech becomes husky as a result

This living voice, which you wanted to stir up from the bosom of the German language, has become husky. Will someone be found who can still hear it?"

This question makes the last words of the Jerusalem address tremble (cf. Gershom G. Scholem, "L'achèvement de la traduction de la Bible par Martin Buber," a speech given at Jerusalem in February 1961, in *Le messianisme juif: Essais sur la spiritualité du judaïsme*, trans. Bernard Dupuy [Paris: Calman-Lévy, 1974], pp. 441–47).

b. Rosenzweig also recalls the "Jewish" languages constituted by Judeo-Spanish and Yiddish when *spoken effectively.*

c. Rosenzweig finally recalls sacred language, the language of prayer, which remains a language *proper* to the Jewish people when they practice, read, and understand it—at least in the liturgy.

Now, to remain with the thus-privileged taxonomic viewpoint, the typical situation of the Franco-Maghrebian Jew that I am trying to describe is one in which, to underline it again, expropriation extends to the loss of these *three resorts*:

a. "Authentic" French (a French ostensibly "maternal" was, perhaps, at his disposal, but it was not metropolitan, only a French *of the colonized*—something the German of Rosenzweig, as well as that of all the Ashkenazic Jews of Europe, was not);

b. Judeo-Spanish (which was no longer practiced);

c. the sacred language, which, more often than not, where it was still used [*prononcée*] in prayer, was neither authentically nor widely taught, nor therefore understood, except in exceptional cases.

2. Arendt. The linguistic ethics of the German Jew who was Rosenzweig was not that of the German Jewish woman named Hannah Arendt. No recourse for her to either a sacred language or a new idiom like Yiddish, but an ineradicable attachment to a unique mother tongue, German. (To a limited extent, which we will not analyze here, her experience would be analogous to that of Adorno. In *Was ist Deutsch?* [which was initially, in 1965, a radio talk; French trans. M. Jimenez and E. Kaufholz, in *Modèles critiques* (Paris: Payot, 1984), pp. 220 ff.], Adorno gives us to understand that he did not take the constraint of English and linguistic exile very well—an exile that, unlike Arendt, he interrupted by returning to Germany, where he could rediscover a language in which he never ceases to recognize a "metaphysical privilege" [p. 229].)

The famous declarations of Arendt on this subject in "Was bleibt? Es bleibt die Muttersprache," a talk with Günter Gaus which was aired by German television in 1964, won a prize and, what is noteworthy, a German prize, the Adolf Grimme prize, are well-known; the talk was published in Munich in Günter Gaus, *Zur Person*, and in French translation as "Qu'est-ce qui reste?: Reste la langue maternelle" in *La tradition cachée: Le Juif comme paria*, trans. Sylvie Courtine-Denamy (Paris: Christian Bourgois, 1987). Arendt responds in a way that is at once disarmed, naïve, and learned when she is interrogated about her attachment to the German language. Did she survive exile in America, her teaching, and her publications in Anglo-American, "even in the bitterest of times"? "Always," she said, plainly and without hesitation. The reply seems initially to consist in one word, *immer*. She always kept this unfailing attachment and this absolute familiarity. The "always" precisely seems to qualify this time of language. Perhaps it says more: not only that the language called maternal is *always* there, *the* "always there," the "always already there," and "always still there," but also that there is perhaps no experience of the "always" and the "same" there, as such, except where there is, if not language, at least some trace which allows itself to be represented by language: as if the experience of the "always" and loyalty to the other as to oneself presupposed the unfailing fidelity to language; even perjury, lying, and infidelity would still presuppose *faith in language*; I cannot lie without believing and making believe in language, without giving credence to the idiom.

After having said "always," very simply, as if the answer were sufficient and exhausted, Arendt, however, adds a few words when confronted with an insistent question about what happened to her habitation of the language in those "bitterest of times," at the time of Nazism at its most unleashed (most unleashed as such, unleashed as Nazism, for there is *always* a time of Nazism before and after Nazism):

"Always. I was telling myself: What is to be done? It is not really the

German language, after all, that has gone mad. And in the second place, nothing can replace the mother tongue" ("Qu'est-ce qui reste?" p. 240).

These *two sentences*, apparently simple and spontaneous, follow each other naturally, without their author seeing—without, at any rate, her giving to see—the abyss opening up under them. Under them or between them.

We cannot return to all the twists and turns of these classic statements. Like "maternal solicitude," which is, as Rousseau said, not "supplemented," *nothing*, Arendt confirms, *can replace the mother tongue*. But how can one think this supposed uniqueness—singularity, irreplaceability—of the mother (indestructible fantasy accredited by the second sentence) together with this strange question about a madness of language, an envisioned delirium excluded by the first sentence?

When Arendt seems, in an interrogation followed by an exclamation, to deny, as an absurdity, the idea that a language can become mad ("I was telling myself: What is to be done? It is not really the German language, after all, that has gone mad"), what is she doing? She is not denying, she is disclaiming. [*Elle ne nie pas, elle dénie.*] She is visibly seeking to reassure herself, in the exclamation of a "not really . . . after all!" "I shall never be made to believe that, in spite of everything!" First of all, she seems to think, commonsensically, that a language in itself can be neither reasonable nor delirious: a language cannot become insane; it cannot be given health care or placed in analysis; it cannot be committed to a psychiatric institution. To allege the dementia of a language, one has to be mad or to be seeking alibis. Hence commonsense whispers this incredulous protestation to Arendt: it is not really language, after all, that has gone mad; that does not make any sense, it is extravagant, who could be made to believe it? Hence it is the subjects of this language, humans themselves, who are losing their minds: Germans, certain Germans who were once masters of the country and that language. Only those people had at that time become diabolical and frenetic. They have no power over the language. It is older than they; it will survive them and will continue to be spoken by Germans who will no longer be Nazis, even by non-Germans. Hence the logical result, the same commonsense which links the second sentence to the first, namely, that the mother tongue cannot be replaced.

Now what Arendt seems not to envisage at all, what she seems to avoid, disclaim, or foreclose, in the most natural way possible, is, in a word, more than one thing:

a. On the one hand, that a language can, in itself, become mad, even a madness, madness itself, the place of madness, madness in the law. Arendt is not willing or able to think this aberration: in order for the "subjects" of a language to become "mad," perverse, or diabolical, evil with a radical evil, it was indeed necessary that language have a hand in it; it must have had its share in what made that madness possible; a non-speaking being, a being without a "mother" tongue cannot become "mad," perverse, wicked, murderous, criminal, or diabolical; and if language is for them something other than a simple, neutral, and external instrument (which Arendt is right to assume, for it is necessary that language be something more and other than a simple tool in order to remain all the time, "always," with oneself through displacements and exiles), it is indeed necessary that the speaking citizen become mad *in* a mad language — in which the same words lose or pervert their so-called commonsense. And we will understand less than nothing in something like Nazism if, along with language and speech, we exclude everything that is inseparable from it: it is not nothing, it is almost everything.

b. On the other hand, and for the same reason, it is necessary for a mother, the mother of the language called "maternal," to be able to become, or to have been, mad (amnesiac, aphasic, delirious). Whereas she should have been led there by her very subject (the irreplaceable uniqueness of the mother tongue), what Arendt does not seem, more profoundly, to have in sight even from very far off, what she did not perhaps *wish* to see, *could* not wish to see, is that it is possible to have a demented mother, a mother "unique" and demented, demented because unique, in the logic of the phantasm. Even if a mother *is* not demented, can one not *have* a demented mother?

This terrible hypothesis can be stated in several ways. One among them would lead us back to the great question of the phantasm, the question of the imagination as *phantasia* and as the place of the *phantasma*. In order to remain close to the Rousseau of the "maternal solicitude that does not supplement [*suppléé*] at all" we could, for example, tie this thematic of (phantasmatic) imagination together with that of compassion. The one and the other, the one as well as the other faculty seem coextensive with supplementarity, that is, with the power of supplementing, of superadding by replacing, therefore with a certain way of replacing the irreplaceable: for example and *par excellence* the mother, where there are grounds to supply the non-suppliable. There is no maternity that does not appear subject to substitution, within the logic or threat of substitution. The idea that one "naturally" knows who the mother is, unlike the father, at the spectacle of birth is an old fantasy [*phantasme*] (still at work in the Freud of *The Ratman*), one that we should not have waited for "surrogate mothers" and "assisted births" to identify as such, namely as a phantasm [*phantasme*]. Let us recall that strange name that someone I do not know (Voltaire says it is Malebranche) gave to imagination: "*the lunatic lady of the house*" ["la folle du logis"]. The mother can become the madwoman of the home, the lunatic of the cell, of the place of substitution where one's home [*le chez-soi*] is lodged, the cell or the place, the locality or location of one's *home* [*le chez-soi*]. It can happen that a mother becomes mad, and that can certainly be a moment of terror. When a mother loses her reason and common sense, the experience of it is as frightening as when a king becomes mad. In both cases, what becomes mad is something like the law or the origin of meaning (the father, the king, the queen, the mother). Now that can sometimes happen, no doubt, as an event, and, one day, once upon a time, in the history of the house or the lineage, threaten the very order of one's home [*chez-soi*], of the house [*casa*], and of the home [*chez*]. This experience can cause anguish like a thing that happens but could possibly not have happened: it even *ought* not to have happened.

But the same thing can be said in two more radical senses, at once different and not different from this one: namely, that (1) formally, the mother as unique and unsuppliable but always subject to substitution, precisely as the place of language, is what makes madness possible; and

(2) more profoundly, as such an always-open possibility, she *is* madness itself, a madness always at work; the mother as the mother tongue, the very experience of absolute uniqueness that can only be replaced *because* it is irreplaceable, translatable because untranslatable, where she is untranslatable (what would be translated otherwise?), the mother *is* madness; the "unique" mother (let us say maternity, the experience of the mother, the relationship to the "unique" mother) is *always* a madness and hence, as the mother and the place of madness, always mad. As mad as the One of the unique. A mother, a relationship with the mother, a maternity is always unique and hence always a place of madness (nothing drives one crazier than the absolute uniqueness of the One or of the She-One [*l'Une*]). But since she is always unique, she is always only re-placeable, re-placeable, suppliable only where there is no unique place except for her. A replacement of the very place, in the place of the place: *khōra*. The tragedy and law of replacement is that it replaces the unique — the unique as the substitute subject to substitution. Whether one is a son or daughter, each time in a different way depending on whether one is a son or daughter, one is always crazy about a mother who is always crazy about that of which she is the mother without ever being able to be uniquely that, precisely at the place, and in the main house [*logis*] of the unique home [*chez-soi*]. And subject to substitution because unique. It could be demonstrated that absolute uniqueness renders one as crazy as absolute replaceability, the absolute replaceability which replaces the emplacement itself, the site, the place, the main house of one's home [*le logis du chez-soi*], the *ipse*, the being-home [*l'être-chez-soi*], or the being-with-oneself of the self.

This discourse on insanity brings us nearer to an energy of madness that could well be linked to the essence of hospitality as the essence of the home [*chez-soi*], the essence of the being-oneself [*l'être-soi*], or of ipseity as being-at-home [*l'être-chez-soi*]. But also as what identifies the Law with the mother tongue, implanting it or at any rate inscribing it therein.

"Always. I was telling myself: What is to be done? It is not really the German language, after all, that has gone mad. And in the second

place [in the second place!], nothing can replace the mother tongue."
After having indicated the irreplaceable, the unsuppliable, of the mother
tongue, Arendt adds: "One can forget their mother tongue, that is true.
I have examples of that around me and, moreover, these persons speak
foreign languages much better than I do. I always speak with a very
heavy accent, and often I happen not to express myself in an idiomatic
fashion. They are, conversely, capable of it, but there we are dealing with
a language in which one cliché expels the other because the productivity
that one shows in one's own language has been neatly cut off, as one
forgets that language."

The interlocutor then asks her whether this forgetting of the mother
tongue is not the "outcome of a repression." Arendt agrees: Yes, the
forgetting of the mother tongue, the substitution which supplements
[*supplée*] the mother tongue would indeed be the effect of a repression.
Beyond that Arendtian formulation, it could perhaps be said that this
is the place and the very possibility of repression par excellence. Arendt
then names Auschwitz as the cut-off, the cut-off point, the cutting-edge
[*le tranchant*] of repression:

"Yes, very often. I have experienced it near certain persons in a completely distressing manner. You see, what was decisive was the day we
heard news about Auschwitz."

Another way of recognizing and accrediting the obvious: an event
such as "Auschwitz," or the very name which names this event can be
held accountable for *repressions*. The word remains a bit vague, it is
no doubt inadequate but it places us, without mincing words, on the
path of a logic, an economy, a topic which no longer has to do with
the ego and properly subjective consciousness. It reminds us to address
these questions beyond the logic or the phenomenology of consciousness, something which still happens too rarely in the most public sphere
of contemporary discourse.

3. **Levinas.** For Levinas, the ethics of language is still other:
neither that of Rosenzweig, nor that of Adorno, nor that of Arendt. A
different experience, indeed, for someone who wrote, taught, and lived
almost all his life in the French language, whereas Russian, Lithuanian,

German, and Hebrew remained his other familiar languages. There seems to be little solemn reference to a mother tongue in his works and no self-assurance assumed in proximity with it, except for the gratitude he expressed, on behalf of someone who declared that "the essence of language is friendship and hospitality," to the French language on each occasion, to French as an adopted or elected language, the welcoming language, the language of the host. In the course of a conversation (Why are such serious things often spoken about on the occasion of public conversations, as if the speakers were caught off guard and spoke in a kind of improvisation?), Levinas names a soil of the soil, the "soil of this language which, for me, is French soil." (François Poirié, *Emmanuel Levinas, qui êtes-vous?* [Lyon: La Manufacture, 1987]). At issue is the classical French of the Enlightenment. By choosing a language which has a soil at its disposal, Levinas speaks of an *acquired* familiarity: the latter has nothing originary about it, it is not maternal in its figure. A radical and typical suspicion, a kind of prudence one would anticipate from Levinas, in the place of what one could call Arendtian radicalism, namely, the attachment to a certain *sacrality* of the *root*. (Levinas always distinguishes holiness from sacrality—in Hebrew even if it is difficult to do that in other languages, German, for example.) As the Heideggerian she remains in this respect, but like many Germans, Jewish or not, Arendt reaffirms the mother tongue, that is to say, a language upon which a virtue of originality is bestowed. "Repressed" or not, this language remains the ultimate essence of the soil, the foundation of meaning, the inalienable property that one carries within oneself. Levinas grants what he says about French in his/its own history first to the language of philosophy. The language of Greek affiliation is capable of accommodating all meaning from elsewhere, even from a Hebraic revelation. Which is another way of saying that language, and above all the "maternal" idiom, is not the originary and irreplaceable place of meaning: a proposition that is, indeed, consistent with Levinasian thought of the hostage and substitution. But language is "expression" rather than generation or foundation: "At no time was Western philosophy losing, in my view, its right to the last word; everything must indeed be *ex-*

pressed in its language [in the heritage of the Greek language], but it is perhaps not the place of the first meaning of beings" (*Ethique et infini* [Paris: Fayard, 1982], p. 15, my italics).

How are we to understand this frequent injunction in Levinas? Why would it be necessary to break, in a certain way, with the root or with the presumed natural or sacred originariness of the mother tongue? No doubt, to break with idolatry and sacredness [*sacralisation*], and to oppose the holiness of the law to them. But is it not also a call to become disillusioned with maternal madness in the name of the paternal holy law (even though the presence of the *schekhina* is also feminine)? In the name of a father who, moreover, is not, as Rosenzweig recalls, fixed to the land? As for the uniqueness of paternal language, one should essentially be able to repeat what we were saying earlier about maternal language and its law. One will have to admit that father and mother are those "legal fictions" that *Ulysses* reserves to paternity: at once replaceable and irreplaceable.

There are some great writers whom I will not hasten to inscribe in the outline of this little taxonomy. First of all, Kafka and Celan. A note would not suffice even to name what these non-Germans (different in that way from Rosenzweig, Scholem, Benjamin, Adorno, Arendt) who wrote especially in German have made happen to the German language. Let it suffice to mark this diacritic value, in a way, between destinies; for Kafka and Celan who were not Germans, German was nevertheless neither a language of adoption nor one of election (the matter was, as we know, more complicated), nor, unlike French for the Jews of Algeria, a "colonial" language, nor a "language of the master." One can perhaps speak, at least, of what Kafka called one day, in an enigmatic but so troubled and troubling way, "the vague approval of fathers": "In German, the average class of language is but ashes, ashes that cannot take on a semblance of life except when searched by excessively lively Jewish hands. . . . What the majority of those who began to write in German wanted was to quit Judaism, generally with the vague approval of fathers (it was this vagueness that was revolting); they wanted it, but their hind legs still stuck to the Judaism of the father, and their forelegs could not find any new terrain. The despair that followed constituted their inspiration" (letter to Max Brod, June 1921, cited by Hanns Zichler, "Kafka va au cinéma," *Cahiers du cinéma*, 1996, Diffusion Seuil, O. Mannoni, p. 165). Since we are following Kafka to the cinema, let us pause briefly over an image: we are in central Europe, let us wonder what the plot is—what matchmaker, what marriage of convenience, could have linked the German of a mother tongue which would not by any means have "gone mad," the German of Hannah Arendt, with the German of Kafka, as of those "who began to write in German" and to "quit Judaism, generally, with the vague approval of fathers." Kafka and Arendt: neither an endogamy nor exogamy of language. Reason or madness?

In this typo-topology, but also outside it, in this place of defiance for the distinction between Ashkenazim and Sephardim, I feel even less capable of a discourse that will measure up to another poetics of language, to an immense and exemplary event: in the work of Hélène Cixous, and in a miraculously unique way, another intersection is weaving *all* these filiations, regenerating them toward a future still without a name. It is necessary to recall that this great-French-Sephardic-Jewish-woman-writer-from-Algeria, who is reinventing, among others, the language of her father, *her* French language, an unheard-of French language, is also a German-Ashkenazic-Jewish-woman through her "mother tongue."

10. Abdelkebir Khatibi, "Incipits," *Du bilinguisme*, p. 189.

11. Contrary to what some theoreticians of the promise as "speech act" and performative language would certainly say, it is not necessary for this promise to be tenable, or even sincerely or seriously held to be tenable, in order for it to be properly what it is. In order for a promise to launch itself forward as such (which therefore implies liberty, responsibility, and decidability), it is necessary for it to be capable, beyond any program of constraint, of allowing itself to be haunted by the possibility, precisely, of its perversion (its conversion into a menace there where a promise can only promise good things, the nonserious commitment of an untenable promise, etc.). This possibility-virtuality is irreducible and calls for another logic of the virtual. I take the liberty of referring, once again, to "Avances."

Cultural Memory | *in the Present*

Rodolphe Gasché, *Of Minimal Things: Studies on the Notion of Relation*

Sarah Winter, *Freud and the Institution of Psychoanalytic Knowledge*

Samuel Weber, *The Legend of Freud*, second edition

Aris Fioretos, ed., *The Solid Letter: Readings of Friedrich Hölderlin*

J. Hillis Miller / Manuel Asensi, *Black Holes / J. Hillis Miller; or, Boustrophedonic Reading*

Miryam Sas, *Fault Lines: Cultural Memory and Japanese Surrealism*

Peter Schwenger, *Fantasm and Fiction: On Textual Envisioning*

Didier Maleuvre, *Museum Memories: History, Technology, Art*

Jacques Derrida, *Monolingualism of the Other; or, The Prosthesis of Origin*

Andrew Baruch Wachtel, *Making a Nation, Breaking a Nation: Literature and Cultural Politics in Yugoslavia*

Niklas Luhmann, *Love as Passion: The Codification of Intimacy*

Mieke Bal, ed., *The Practice of Cultural Analysis: Exposing Interdisciplinary Interpretation*

Jacques Derrida and Gianni Vattimo, eds., *Religion*

Library of Congress Cataloging-in-Publication Data
Derrida, Jacques.
  [Monolinguisme de l'autre, ou, La prothèse d'origine. English]
  Monolingualism of the other; or, The prosthesis of origin /
Jacques Derrida ; translated by Patrick Mensah.
      p.   cm.   — (Cultural memory in the present)
  ISBN-10: 0-8047-3288-4 (cloth : alk. paper)
  ISBN-13: 978-0-8047-3288-8 (cloth : alk. paper)
  ISBN-10: 0-8047-3289-2 (pbk : alk. paper)
  ISBN-13: 978-0-8047-3289-5 (pbk : alk. paper)
  1. Language and languages — Philosophy.   I. Title.   II. Series.
  P106.D456613   1998
  401—dc21   98-4454
                                                                CIP

This book is printed on acid-free paper.
Original printing 1998